Praise for *Giving Grief Meaning*

"Lily Dulan had to bear the unbearable, a loss that is every parent's nightmare. This book relays her journey from the valley of excruciating pain to a peaceful life on the other side of it. She began the journey not knowing if peace would ever be hers again. She was rewarded for each step she took in trying to find it, discovering keys that indeed unlocked the way for her and which now she can share with others. For those still in earlier phases of grief, this book illuminates some mysterious ways a broken heart can heal."

—Marianne Williamson, author, teacher, and activist

"Death and loss are potent experiences that can overwhelm a person for life. This could have been the fate of Lily Dulan after her beloved newborn daughter Kara unexpectedly died. Her moving account of how her daughter's memory eventually led her to a life's vocation of helping others is a testament to the resilience of the human spirit."

—Sharon Salzberg, author of *Real Happiness and Real Love*

"Lily Dulan has written a courageous book filled with depth and vulnerability. Through the devastating loss of her beloved daughter Kara, Lily was inspired to create the process of 'The Name Work.' I'm sure that it will prove to be an accessible and useful tool for many people to give meaning to their grief. This book is filled with real-world examples of love overcoming despair. Lily encourages the reader to feel their own truth and develop empowering thoughts in sync with that truth. For all who are grieving, this book fulfills its promise to bring readers a sense of renewal, love, and ultimate peace of mind."

—Judith Orloff, MD, author of *The Emp͏~ ͏ ͏al Guide*

"Insurmountable pain strikes deep and transforms lives; the effects last a lifetime. How we engage that pain truly determines our path forward. Through *Giving Grief Meaning*, the reader journeys with Lily Dulan as she blossoms into the unique, stunning, beautiful, and giving person that she is today. To take pain and truly transform it toward enlightened joy and giving for others is a gift. We at the Unatti Foundation are truly grateful for the wisdom that Lily has imparted to our girls in Nepal. The dedication of the Kara Love Project Community Room is a true testament to the care that Lily provides to raise the human spirit. Lily is now sharing all the possibilities to turn pain into growth with the world. Brava!"

—Stephanie Waisler Rubin and Michelle Armoni,
Unatti Foundation

"Grief hits us all at some point in our lives—it knows no boundaries. How we respond to it can determine whether it stops us from living or deepens our connection to ourselves and those around us. Lily's personal experience with grief has left her with profound wisdom about how to cope with this most painful—but most human—aspect of life. *Giving Grief Meaning* shares guidance and practical advice for living with loss or any kind of trauma. She shares incredible yet tangible healing modalities in this book, which offers insight into the complicated journey of grieving in an authentic and honest way. I'm so grateful Lily found a way to give her experience a voice and to create this gift for the rest of us. Highly recommended!"

—Maggie Lin, founder of Foster Nation

"Lily Dulan has emerged from the pain of an unimaginable loss with a desire to contribute to the good of others. She transforms her grief, daily, into acts of love through support of organizations that are in service to young people. Through them, and through her other good works, the memory of Kara is honored."

—Lynn Warshafsky, founding director of Venice Arts

"Lily's book, *Giving Grief Meaning*, takes the reader on an intimate personal journey of Lily's experience of what it is like to have a much loved and wanted baby in the NICU, and then for her sweet baby Kara to die of SIDS eight weeks after birth at home. Lily and her husband were shattered by unfathomable grief and trauma. Lily's assumptive world was blown up and she shares her authentic, messy, and dark despair of grief. With the help of community and a strong spiritual practice, she was able to transform her pain and suffering into helping herself and others. She chose to live and thrive through her love for Kara. Grief is LOVE. Lily created The Name Work, and a foundation in Kara's memory, called the Kara Love Project. The Name Work is a beautiful deck of cards with an initial on it. It is a heart-centered 'tool' or process to create affirmations, positive attributes and describe a loved one by using the letters of their name. Brilliant! There's a quote I like to share, 'Death ends life, not a relationship.' We continue to create bonds, rituals, and connection with the deceased—because we love them so deeply. I cannot recommend this healing book enough to anyone suffering through the wide range and turbulent human emotions of grief, no matter the type of loss. This book will help validate and normalize the lifelong ups and downs of the grieving process. Thank you, Lily, for your gift of this book and choosing life—you are helping so many by shining your light, grace and love with us all."

   —Ivy Love Margulies, PsyD, clinical psychologist specializing in
      grief and infant loss

"Lily Dulan has experienced a parent's worst nightmare, the loss of her beloved daughter Kara. In her book *Giving Grief Meaning* she has so tenderly yet courageously given a voice to the grief and sorrow we all experience in this human journey. Through the sharing of her personal experience with her touch love kindness, she helps us to navigate through grief and come out the other side as a more full and awake human being. This should be a required reading for all humans."

   —Govind Das, director of Bhakti Yoga Shala

"Thank you for sharing your story of grief and loss. In a world where so many people are hurting, we need honest, authentic voices speaking their truth and sharing their stories of overcoming with others. The Name Work provides us with a valuable tool to help heal, grow, transform, and reach our highest potential. I look forward to sharing this tool with others in the mental wellness community."

—Metta World Peace, NBA Champion and mental
　wellness advocate

"Lily has transformed heart-wrenching grief into a method of healing which she calls The Name Work. In many ways, her permutations of names are reminiscent of the deepest mystical name meditations of the Kabbalists—and intuitively picks up on those transformative traditions. And yet her work is very practical: she offers concrete tools for facing the hardships which inevitably confront us. For those looking to shift their grief toward growth, while continuing to acknowledge it, this book offers a clear path."

—Rabbi Andrew Hahn, PhD (The "Kirtan Rabbi")

"Lily Dulan has written an important book that is both highly informative and practical. Her approach is also deeply spiritual, gently enabling even those who don't feel particularly nimble in that realm. Speaking from her own devastating and tragic experience of the death of her young daughter, Ms. Dulan weaves together her various arenas of expertise, giving others the tools to work through their grief in ways that are both honest and constructive. Ms. Dulan's approach to the process of grieving is that it is real, and rather than it being something to overcome, we can mold it into a force for good, for ourselves, and everyone we meet. In doing so, the lives of those we loved and continue to love, never end."

—Neil Comess-Daniels, Rabbi Emeritus, Beth Shir Shalom

Giving Grief
MEANING

Giving Grief
MEANING

A Method for Transforming Deep Suffering into Healing and Positive Change

by Lily Dulan

mango
PUBLISHING GROUP

Coral Gables

Published by Mango Publishing Group, a division of Mango Media Inc.

Cover Design: Gabrielle Mechaber
Layout & Design: Morgane Leoni
Cover Art: © Torie Zalben

For permission requests, please contact the publisher at:
Mango Publishing Group
2850 S Douglas Road, 2nd Floor
Coral Gables, FL 33134 USA
info@mango.bz

For special orders, quantity sales, course adoptions and corporate sales, please email the publisher at sales@mango.bz. For trade and wholesale sales, please contact Ingram Publisher Services at customer.service@ingramcontent.com or +1.800.509.4887.

Giving Grief Meaning: A Method for Transforming Deep Suffering into Healing and Positive Change

Library of Congress Cataloging-in-Publication number: 2020946330
ISBN: (print) 978-1-64250-313-5, (ebook) 978-1-64250-314-2
BISAC category code SEL010000, SELF-HELP / Death, Grief, Bereavement

Printed in the United States of America

In loving memory of our precious daughter,

Kara Meyer Dulan

May 22, 2009 to July 29, 2009

And to my earth angels David, Marcelle, and Sally

Contents

Foreword

It is with great pleasure that I write this foreword for Lily Dulan's debut work, *Giving Grief Meaning*. Lily and I have known each other for more than fifteen years. In that time, I have witnessed the birth of an incredible woman, a true visionary, and an authentic leader who has put the spiritual principles we teach at Agape International Spiritual Center into practice. That birth and transformation was not without pain and sorrow, not without heartbreaking loss and grief. In fact, it is often major and seemingly insurmountable obstacles that enable us to realize our highest potential and imbue life with greater meaning and purpose. While Lily's journey is no exception to that edict, the work she's developed as a result is exceptional and a powerful way for others to find meaning and peace in the face of trauma and grief.

I came to know Lily more intimately when I was asked to give a retreat with the late Ram Dass in Hawaii. It was there, away from the hustle and bustle of the city, that we really had time to be together. At the time, she was pregnant with her daughter Kara, and we were overjoyed that her vision of becoming a mother had become manifest. Lily and her husband David had tried to conceive for years, and the birth of Kara was a gift that our community celebrated. Very shortly thereafter, however, I helped them release her from this earth. Lily, as one can only imagine, was devastated and traumatized to her core with grief. She was not sure she could go on. It was then that I took Lily's hands in mine and said, "You are at a crossroads and have a choice about what comes next. You can choose to grow from this tragedy, or you can choose to shrink, to withdraw from life and fade away. The question now, my friend, is what do you choose?"

Whether she knew it then or not, Lily chose to grow.

While the process and timing are different for everyone, transformation can and does occur. It is my belief that the potential, the vision, is always bigger than the pain. Ultimately the pain will push you until a vision finally pulls you.

As Lily processed Kara's death, she was drowned by relentless and colossal waves of pain, torrents of grief, and even whispers of heartache until the vision for her new project, The Name Work, pulled her from grave despair. Pain kept knocking at her door, pushing it open, until her purpose pulled her from her pain so she could move in the direction of peace.

To be human means you will experience suffering, pain, and trauma. It is our relationship to suffering and our ability to transform the pain that gives meaning to life. We become worthy of our suffering when we are able to use it for transformation.

Today, Lily keeps Kara alive in her heart. She shifted the energy around her suffering in ways that kept her going and making her work bigger, better, and brighter for other people who are going through similar situations. Lily's work continues beyond The Name Work with a foundation she created in her daughter's name, the Kara Love Project, which helps marginalized individuals and communities rise to their potential.

If you're experiencing pain or loss, The Name Work, a process in which you create affirmations and positive qualities around your name or the name of a loved one, is a wonderful tool and practice for handling and moving through trauma and grief. It offers a beautiful method for transforming your pain to make room for the vision and potential that is your true calling for a bigger and brighter life.

Abundant Peace and Blessings,

—Michael Bernard Beckwith
Founder and Spiritual Director, Agape International
Spiritual Center
Author, *Life Visioning and Spiritual Liberation*

PROLOGUE

In Loving Memory of Kara Meyer Dulan

May 22–July 29, 2009

These pages are written in beloved memory of our daughter, Kara Meyer Dulan, who didn't have the chance to grow into her name. As soon as she came, she was gone. My tiny baby disappeared. Poof. A cruel kind of magic. She exited this world in the pitch dark of night, when the noisy urban traffic jams recede and the chirps of crickets can be heard in our canyon. In the pause that the wee hours create, the coyotes come out in search of prey and wild things reign supreme. Now, all we had left was Kara's name and memories of her very short life.

Before she left us, the calm of night felt extra special, since we had been in our new home for only two months. When we moved in, I couldn't wait to nest, especially since I had spent the last few months living at Cedars-Sinai Medical Center, due to a complicated pregnancy. I missed our new home and the beauty of our canyon. I was anxious to leave that skinny hospital bed with interloping nurses and the general clanks and beeps of life-or-death matters.

Returning home, the long drive with its tall trees seemed like an entrance to Shangri-La. Tucked in behind our iron gates, we felt safe and sound. *It was time,* I told myself. David and I had left our days of crazy partying behind and our quiet canyon provided the ideal atmosphere for raising a child. How grateful I was to surrender to the predictable pulse of life. I paused to take in my surroundings and wondered, *Why did we wait so long?* Lying there snuggled up in my blanket, feeling the day move into night, I listened to the distant hum of cars on Sunset Boulevard. I had just bathed and fed Kara, and I was ready for a few hours of sleep before the next feeding. It was a gift, lying in our new wide bed, our sweet baby in her crib next to us, surrendering to the quiet. It all felt predictable and sensible.

Later that night, all semblance of order ceased. Our precious baby girl was taken before the birds came to usher in the light. I had a strange dream that night that angels and celestial beings came to me and said that they were taking my baby to another realm. In the dream, I stood at the entrance to a heavenly place filled with golden light. I didn't feel horror. Rather, I was filled with peace and otherworldly understanding.

I remember seeing the great trunk of Ganesh, the elephant-headed god, remover of obstacles. In my dream, he was being absorbed into the Wailing Wall of Jerusalem. I stood in front of what looked like the wall of the Second Temple, a place fit for Saint Peter. Was I seeing an entrance to heaven? I watched in dream-like awe, standing there in the golden light.

One brief moment later, a great cosmic *whoosh* reverberated in my ears and woke me up. It was louder than the sound of a castle gate crashing down, more intense than human ears could handle. My sense of peace evaporated. It felt like I was being shot out of a portal when I awoke to David's screams. "Lily, Lily, Kara is gone!" He was trying to revive her by doing mouth-to-mouth resuscitation. I didn't have the heart to stop him, but I knew it was too late. Her face was already streaked with death.

Kara left this world on July 29, 2009. She was two months old. They named the cause of death SIDS and our lives were shattered. The kind-eyed coroner was sure to let us know that her sleep area, without pillows and blankets, had been perfect. There was nothing we could have done. No way to roll back the darkness.

Introduction

A decade after Kara's death, I feel ready to share my story. As strange as it may seem, I have found a way to see Kara's untimely death as one of my life's greatest teachings. Although I would do anything to have her back in my arms, my life's purpose was birthed through coming to terms with my loss and finding a way to use Kara's name to heal. Today, my world is filled with many gifts, as my husband and I have adopted two girls. I feel more sensitive, compassionate, and loving than I was before Kara came and went. But it wasn't easy to get here.

That's why I'm writing this book—to offer people experiencing grief, loss, and suffering a concrete way to move through life's challenges, trauma, and what may seem like insurmountable obstacles. I believe that we have to learn to get more in touch with our suffering and really feel it before we can create positive meaning that will assist us in our healing. Ever since my daughter's death, countless people have shared their pain with me. I have seen that, when they feel connected to my grief, they become more in touch with their own as they search for a way to heal and move through life.

My healing journey has been long and difficult at times, but an ultimately fulfilling process. I walked through the valley of the shadow of death, and I have discovered a way to maneuver through the worst parts of life. In the pages that follow, I will be sharing the methods that allowed me to grieve, to heal, and to find meaning, hope, and perspective once again. During that dark period, I created a method that helped me when I was searching for meaning and trying desperately to come to terms with losing my child.

I call my discovery *The Name Work*. It involves assigning positive attributes and important qualities to each letter in your name or the name of a loved one. In this way, I hope you can find meaning in the most challenging of times. It worked for me. This is what it looks like:

KARA
K stands for Kindness.
A stands for Alignment.
R stands for Regeneration.
A stands for Action.

The four qualities which I found in Kara's name are universal and apply to everyone's life. Throughout the pages of this book, we will delve deeper into the name Kara and the qualities associated with each letter. Working with the letters in her name, I will guide you through The Name Work method. It involves the use of breath, movement, writing exercises, active questioning, and positive self-talk. I believe that the qualities I have discovered are sacred and can help each and every one of us live a more centered, meaningful, energetic, and fulfilled life.

I will also share with you how you can apply this method to your own name, a new name that you create, or the name of a loved one. Once you become comfortable with accessing the qualities found in a name, you will be igniting those attributes to add meaning and purpose to your life.

A word of caution: Creating a sense of centeredness, peace, and direction doesn't mean things won't get messy or sad. They will. Grief and obstacles come and go like the seasons, and to push our feelings away only takes us deeper into despair. But as you access eye-opening and light-filled qualities in the associated letters, it will become easier to give birth to your purpose.

Have you ever noticed that the most exotic vacation spots are the hardest to reach? They require boats, planes, and treks through the mud. When you are available to do The Name Work, you are traveling to exotic places within you. They may seem difficult to reach at first, but once you begin the process, the journey itself is extremely rewarding.

I wrote this book for anyone who wants to face their grief and understand and release past traumas, blockages, addictions, and phobias. My journey from agony to rebirth has taken many years of surrender, deep introspection, and self-healing in order to create a solid foundation for The Name Work. My aim is to help you embrace your grief, loss, or pain and help you discover the expanded possibilities that lie deep within. While some wounds may appear worse than others, we all suffer. It's part of the human condition.

This book is a guide to finding new purpose in your life by embodying the beauty and power of a name. It can give meaning to your life and your personal struggle. It can give you the tools to dig deeper so you'll be better equipped to love yourself and live with compassion and understanding. My experience has taught me that trying to escape pain leads to more pain. We all have our poisons and pitfalls. Whether it's drink, drugs, social media addiction, bad television, or junk food, the comfort these vices give us is short-lived and has left me and countless others stuck in a swamp of anger, depression, and self-loathing. Looking within and touching our shared humanity, wounds and all, makes life that much sweeter.

I invite you to try my Name Work method to help you move through whatever is holding you back from living your fullest life. I offer you these pages with an open heart, praying that, through The Name

Work, you will discover the tools that can help you find a sense of renewal, love, and peace of mind.

Warmly,
Lily

PART I

CHAPTER 1

Losing Kara

On the night we lost Kara, I can still see myself running out to meet the glaring lights of Fire Truck 19 in my soft pink bathrobe. The one I wore in the hospital. The one I was wearing when I fed Kara and put her down to sleep. It had been a couple of months since I'd hoisted myself down from my hospital bed and waddled like a mama duck in that same soft robe, ignoring the jabbing pain from my Cesarean section. I made my way down the long, shiny hospital hallways to the NICU where Kara spent her first week of life. A week later, she was in our new home. The experts said she was perfectly healthy by then. It was a wicked trick.

"Hurry! Hurry! We don't have enough time!" I told the EMT who had answered our call. Like my husband David, I just didn't want to believe she was already gone.

"I'm moving as fast as I can," he snapped.

He was a young guy, and he must have been a rookie because, later, he paced the halls of the hospital, peeking into the office where David and I sat with a grief counselor. I knew he felt guilty for snapping at me. I can still picture him walking back and forth, wringing his hands and hanging his head as I cried in disbelief. He didn't come into the room. There was nothing he could say. There was simply no reviving her.

A few days later, Kara, the love of our life, was swallowed up by the earth, laid to rest in the ground in a cedar box. We were huddling together under the cemetery tent when I took a fistful of earth from

Kara's grave and put it in an empty plastic water bottle. I wanted a piece of her.

At some point in my grief, I scattered the dirt in my yard along with whatever hope I had left. Over the next few months, it felt like the gnarled trees outside my window might take me, too. Or maybe I wished they would. The world was swirling by. There were people jogging by the ocean, holding hands, and laughing, crying, raging, sweating, planning—doing all the things that humans do. But I was motionless. Numbed out. A dead woman walking.

Months earlier, when I was ready to conceive, my yoga teacher, Mark, had suggested I tie a red sash around my belly as a meditative exercise to visualize myself getting pregnant. After David and I drove to the fabric store for just the right color of red silk, I painted a gold picture of the Star of David in the middle of the sash. Then I sprinkled gold glitter on it and blew the excess away. I can still see myself standing in our old carport, sheltered by the tall cypress trees, gold sparkle dust blowing in the wind. The star or *Shree Yantra* represented the life force of male and female energy alike. "The Universal union of opposites." I visualized Kara's birth in that sash, as I went through a series of yoga poses or asanas. I now have that sash stored in a box of keepsakes, and I believe that the commitment I made when I was wearing it lives on.

When Kara was born, we named her in the spirit of *Cara*, which means friendship in Gaelic, for her proud Irish grandmother, Katherine McNamara. I took the K in Katherine and the "ara" sound from McNamara and there it was. The perfect name. A family name. A name fit for a princess.

We gave Kara the middle name Meyer, after her great grandfather on my dad's side. I was too young to know him well, but I remember his contagious smile and his love of books and playing the mandolin. My beautiful grandmother referred to him as Daddy in that "Daddy-O" kind of way, and together they made a gorgeous couple. I was honored to pass on his name as a part of our Jewish tradition.

I don't remember much about our little one, other than the fact that she was born really small, barely five pounds. I wrote down the few memories of her that I savor as proof that she was here. That she was somebody and that she had a name. The young nurse in the NICU called her Tiny and Mighty. The name was fitting as I watched how she clung to life, yellowed with jaundice, a tube in her nose, desperately trying to learn to suck. It was hard for her to latch onto my breast or a bottle, but she finally mastered the art of feeding and began to gain weight. She became my little Butter Bean, my T Buba (tiny baby), hanging on like the rest of us, ready to go home.

When Kara was a solid ten pounds, our pediatrician, Dr. Linda, said she was as healthy as any other baby. On that monumental day, we dressed her in a lavender onesie that read "CUTIE PIE." We put her in her new gray car seat and took the forty-five-minute drive to our quiet canyon. She had a full head of black hair, and I loved gazing into her wrinkle-free face as she looked up at me through a pair of the bluest eyes I'd ever seen.

We sat in my green mid-century womb chair, listening to Creedence Clearwater Revival. *Suzie Q, baby I love you—oh, Suzie Q.* I marveled at Kara. She had the tiniest feet ever. I can still feel their softness. Really, the child was a showstopper. An angel from the start. We would later take home our girls who were born giants by comparison, bald-headed and wrinkled. It took a few months before their worm-like appearance smoothed and you could really see how adorable they were. But not Kara. You could see what she looked like from the start.

She had the same coal-black hair as her dad once had, and she had his cherubic chin. Perhaps this vision of her was a gift, since she wouldn't be around for more than a blip.

I recall putting her in her red stroller and going on a pilgrimage to the local Vedanta temple. I took her on a few trips to family-friendly eateries; we stopped by a Toys R Us for diapers, and we took a trip down to Main Street in Santa Monica to have my hair colored after my long hospital stint. We went to our first "Mommy and Me" baby group at my friend Suzie's home, and we went to a street festival to see a friend play in a rock band. Kara was with me on all of these outings, sitting in her car seat or swaddled in a tan cloth carrier at my breast.

Had it all been too much for her? Should I have kept her at home, away from the elements? Should I have listened to the prenatal doctor, rather than my OB-GYN, and left her in my belly for a week or two longer? My doctor said it was okay to have the C-section, and I was anxious to get out of the hospital. If Kara had incubated longer, would she have survived? *If only I'd left her in longer,* I kept thinking. But my OB-GYN assured me that she was okay.

The night before Kara died, I remember giving her a sponge bath. She loved the warm misty feel of the water, and she smiled at me before I put her down. "Look, David, she's smiling," I said in blissed-out glee. But as soon as she came, she was gone, and the what-ifs and the shoulda-coulda-wouldas tormented me.

How I came back from that dark night of despair, I can't really say. My husband David came back, too. Perhaps it was our living earth angels, our daughters, that gave us a sense of hope. But how we moved forward to go through with the adoptions is a mystery. Suffice it to say, I am here now on a lazy afternoon, writing to tell you that we weren't sucked under, that somehow, the light that is the living spirit allowed us to embrace living again.

CHAPTER 2

The Memorial and the Aftermath

When we buried Kara, the living nightmare began. Despite the peace I had found in my dream the night she died, I was not okay. My baby was gone. I ruminated for years about the possible meaning of that dream. My black-and-white thinking and dualistic religious guilt were out of control. Had I put other gods before me by chanting in Sanskrit in my yoga classes and kirtan chant sessions? Had I gone down the wrong path with my yoga satsang? Was I being punished? When I was in deep grief, my faith evaporated, and I was resistant to many of the strategies that had once offered me comfort. The important thing is that I put one foot in front of the other and never gave up. For me, finding peace and comfort has been an evolving process.

The day after Kara died, Reverend Michael Beckwith, founder of the Agape Spiritual Center, cancelled a trip and spoke at Kara's memorial. His wife, Rickie, sang, and our entire community was in disbelief. Our Bhakti Yoga Satsang was there as well, leading chants as we clung together in collective shock. One week earlier, we'd held a welcoming ceremony for Kara. It had been a joyous occasion, and my husband and I were so proud to show off our baby girl and welcome everyone into our new home. I had sat with Kara in my favorite green womb chair and chanted in tearful joy. When we concluded, my yoga teacher, Mark, had everyone gather on the soft lawn in a circle beneath the stars, and we held hands and cooed over our baby girl.

"Welcome to the world, Kara!" we said. Everyone cheered.

Now we were gathered for a different reason. We were in mourning, and I had to connect to my community to save myself from sinking. I later consulted Rabbi Neil Comess-Daniels, who, like Reverend Michael, would become an important teacher in my life. "Did an angry God take her?" I asked him, tears spilling down my face. "Am I being punished?"

"No," he told me. "Ours is a loving God. You did nothing wrong. Please don't worry yourself."

His assurances offered me no peace. For a long time, I wasn't willing to see the good in our world or in God. A loving God would not have taken my baby. There was no sense or order to my world, but somehow I knew that this attitude would not save me. I would have to let myself off the hook and learn to trust life. I saw grief as an ocean with no way to fathom its depths.

The only way to assign meaning to Kara's short life was for me to choose to live again. My twelve-step sponsor told me to *act as if*. That meant to act as if the world was good. As if God was love. As if I had the courage to make it through. If I persisted in insisting that it was too late, that mankind was depraved, that an angry God had punished me by taking my baby, I wouldn't be able to function.

When I was in the third grade, I remember sitting at my wooden desk in Mrs. Grommet's class, watching an environmental film about a mama dog that lost her pups in a fire. As she howled for her litter, whimpering and running in circles, my heart broke. There was no logic there as I watched the mama dog panting, pacing the dust, searching in vain for her babies.

When I look back on that moment, my womb flutters with the ache of loss. Had I always sensed on some visceral level that I would lose my infant child? I remember that mother pup on many occasions, feeling a silent solidarity with her that transcends body, space, and time.

I have tread many miles since that day in third grade, and still, the darker mysteries of this life only serve to confuse and confound me. I am just as baffled by it all as I was back then. Yet, as my confusion and bewilderment lay heavy on me like sandbags, I knew that gnawing on the bitterness wasn't going to help. I couldn't remain in that spot, waiting it out. I knew I would die there. Simply put, I had to talk it out, feel it as much as I could, and keep moving through it.

At first, all I could do was guard my thoughts, and when the fear set in, I would mutter *I am safe, I am protected.* I recited these broken parts of a prayer in my darkness, afraid of the long hallways in our home that felt haunted. I continued reciting those little parts of the prayer as I struggled through the darkness until I could see what was good and right in the world. I needed to put one foot in front of the other and act as if it would all be okay.

Trudging along that path was bleak, uncertain, and stagnant at times. I was hiking with a friend once when she put her hand on my shoulder and said, "How are you even walking around? I would have died."

I leaned into her, basking in the comfort of friendship, but I didn't have an answer. We walked on for a bit in silence, our feet moving over the same grass Kara's bright red stroller had done, just a few months back. I had hated that stroller. I wanted a nice neutral color, beige or even blue, but David chose red. We had an argument on the first day we took her out in it. Now, it all seemed so petty as I walked, grieving and childless, across the bluffs near our home in the company of a friend.

Today I would do anything to have my baby back and to push her in that red stroller. The one that was too flashy for me. How *had* I survived? I was sluggish and dull, unable to feel much of anything for a long time. Perhaps the fog of grief kept me alive since the numbness was constant.

One night, I was lying in bed, listening to the birds and the crickets, when a wave of deep grief hit me. It happened fast, like a hijacking. I was overcome. The stab of pain was so great, I thought I might die. And then, like a cloud that obscures the sun, the fog set in again.

Some years later, a friend told me she felt like there was something wrong with her because she couldn't feel the death of her husband. I'd been where she was, and I was able to tell her that our nervous systems have a way of shielding us from too much pain. The numbness that we feel is actually our protector. Perhaps it is even God who offers us this fog, giving us only as much as we can tolerate.

I don't know how I got through it. I still don't have a complete answer. All I know is that I was willing to heal, and my pain abated in its own time. I had to give myself the space to heal and acknowledge that there was no right or wrong way to grieve.

One of the hardest parts was that our house, once a Shangri-La, seemed full of malevolence once Kara was gone. The magical trees and natural elements looked as if they could suck me under. I no longer trusted the earth beneath me. I finally understood the title of an old professor's book, *The Myth of Solid Ground*.

The thing is, there are no assurances in this life, and nothing is firm. The solidity of the earth cannot be trusted as the tectonic plates move beneath us. The idea that babies will absolutely live into adulthood is a sham. For me, it was just a matter of time before it all crumbled and

I couldn't see the light at all. I can easily go back to that threatening place, to that ominous feeling that I and everyone else could be taken out without warning. Wham bam, no thank you, ma'am. Over. Kaput.

CHAPTER 3

Finding My Way

It is important for me to acknowledge the fact that there were many seemingly insurmountable obstacles that appeared before Kara died. We all suffer, and getting in touch with that which pains us can inspire us to examine our lives and cultivate an expanded consciousness. Back then, I learned that I needed to be ready and willing to face what troubled me in order to bring our precious daughter into this world. I would ultimately have to quit drinking and undergo all-consuming fertility treatments which were necessary for me to give birth in the first place. Whether or not the drinking affected my ability to get pregnant is a matter of debate.

To be frank, I knew it would be impossible to inject the cocktail of medications the doctor prescribed when I was passed out drunk. One thing was for sure: things needed to shift. Becoming aware of what I needed meant that I had to fundamentally change my life and put a stop to the suffering that I brought on myself and others through addictive behaviors. I used to type with a cigarette dangling from my mouth and one in the ashtray, a glass of wine by my side, fighting off last night's hangover and convincing myself that I was okay because I was in school. My perpetual-student gig hid the fact that I couldn't hold down a job, I was mooching off of my husband and I was playing the role of being perpetually lost and angry. I lived in fear of being a grownup, of truly committing to my husband, of having a child of our own. And so I drowned out the sound of my own biological clock whenever I could, escaping in fantasies of all kinds which would take me nowhere.

I drank for many reasons, but mostly I wanted to numb out. There were half-empty bottles of wine littering our counters, making the place smell like a barroom floor. I always left a little wine in the bottle. Just a quarter of a bottle. That way, I wouldn't have to admit to drinking the entire thing to my husband, the cleaning lady, or even to myself. This is what they call denial. I was completely checked-out back then. I had a string of unsavory diversions that jeopardized my marriage and put my life on the line. It all became too much one night when I was driving drunk and woke up from a blackout far from home. I was flabbergasted that I was still in one piece. "Sick and tired of being sick and tired," I began shopping around for ways to feel better. I would eventually learn that I have to take responsibility for myself, no matter how wrong I am or how *wronged* I feel.

Thank God, during that time, a well-meaning neighbor took me to a twelve-step women's meeting of which I still am a part. I had been to recovery groups before, but never had I felt a sense of belonging like I did there. The women embraced me and valued me until I could value myself. I eventually learned that I had to take stock of my life and examine what I was allowing to hold me back. In twelve-step programs, they call this process of rigorous self-examination "taking a moral inventory."

My list went on and on. I was filled with self-hatred and remorse over the things I'd done and the wrongs that had been done to me. I had said one too many fuck-yous to my family, but I finally learned that holding onto the narrative of "what they did to me" would get me nowhere. It didn't matter if my anger was warranted or not. The rage and sadness left unexamined and unchallenged would not propel me in the direction of my highest vision for a beautiful life. I had to learn to love myself, warts and all. This meant letting others have their opinions of me, negative or otherwise. I've heard it said in wellness and self-help circles many times over: "Would you rather be happy or would you rather be right?" Slowly but surely, I began to choose happy, or at the very least, being at peace.

As time went on, I finally found the willingness to do away with a lifestyle that was killing me. The late motivational author Louise Hay says that "willingness" is all we need for our lives to begin to change.

Having these tools in my toolbox before Kara died helped me with the grieving process later. Still, I had to be willing to come back to self-love and self-forgiveness again and again as I evaluated what I needed to change.

In order to sow the seeds of what would eventually become The Name Work, I had to be willing to move out of my comfort zone. Reverend Michael Beckwith likes to say we can choose to grow or shrink from adversity. For me there was no choice; I had to choose growth or there was a real likelihood that I could have died. I might have snuffed out my life, or worse, hit someone else when I was drunk-driving before Kara came into the world. Who knows what could have happened? I know one thing for certain: had I not gotten sober and become willing to face myself, I would not have been able to conceive Kara or be around to write this today.

Eventually, the pain in my life led me on a spiritual quest and to a master's program in psychology where I began working with a therapist that I stayed with for over a decade. It was difficult being in therapy, and I often wanted to quit. At times, it seemed futile to dredge up the past, yet something in me propelled me forward.

CHAPTER 4

Connecting with Our Trauma

If we have faced trauma, abuse, violence, and/or the death of a loved one, many of our memories of the past may be ugly and dark. We may live in fear of remembering. Science is now showing us that we store grief, loss, and trauma in our bodies, and if we leave our trauma unexamined, we become vulnerable to a host of emotional as well as physical illnesses. The bedrock of The Name Work, a system of healing that I have created, is learning to get in touch with our negative experiences and emotions so we can gain a sense of perspective and learn the art of practicing positivity and kindness. For me, this happens when I pay attention to what I experience physically as well as emotionally. When practiced on a regular basis, the process of getting quiet through meditation and/or yoga, feeling what comes up in your mind and body, and then using your name to create affirmations sheds light on the true power of positivity and affirmative thought.

The sense of purpose and perspective that can be sourced through practicing The Name Work is real and the methods are not new. Dr. Bessel Vander Kolk's seminal research on trauma demonstrates that when we repress anger, grief, and/or trauma, we become ill. His research with war veterans underscores the fact that, when we slow down and are able to touch our own anguish, we can relate to it in new and more loving and compassionate ways. This has been proven to help heal those who have sought a reprieve from violent flashbacks, angry outbursts, grief dissociation, and the like.

When something seemingly grabs us and thrusts us back into a previous state of trauma, it is called a trigger. Those of us who have PTSD or traumatic memories may constantly scan the environment for real or perceived threats. Trying to keep negative experiences at bay may actually keep us stuck and prevent us from embracing the healing journey. Many of us who are on the path of recovery have a habit of pushing away the very things that can help us.

There is no way around the darkness. We must learn to feel it, move through it, and cultivate calm through developing the ability to find spaciousness within. This is the core of The Name Work. Jamaican singer/songwriter Bob Marley sings, "Out of the darkness, aye, must come out the light." When I face my fears, they become smaller. It's like pulling back the curtain in the land of Oz and realizing that the monster is only a cowering little man in an ill-fitting suit. Removing the drape and taking a peek at the control room gives me the aha moment that the bogeyman can't hurt me at all.

I've heard many well-meaning people say that blocking trauma out, like a horse with blinders, and just trotting on is the best way forward. Unfortunately for some of us, it isn't that easy. We can't pretend that life has been a positive experience when we are feeling darkness and despair closing in. Pretending that all is okay when it's not is called "a spiritual bypass." Even worse than pretending that all is well when I am knee-deep in it, some people insist that my own negative thinking about life is what brought on the death of my child. This kind of "toxic positivity" is damaging and just plain wrong.

That said, the science of positivity gets a bad rap these days because of a few irresponsible practitioners blaming victims and telling them they brought the tragedy and/or violence on themselves. These spiritually immature people tell desperate clients it was their "lack of higher consciousness" that made their current horror a reality. In the wake of this "spiritual malpractice," it is understandable that people are fed up and that leaders in the field of grief and trauma are speaking out.

The pitfalls of false positivity are real. Still, it becomes important not to throw away the whole of affirmative science. It has become popular these days to denounce the entire movement and turn our backs on the old adage, "Everything happens for a reason." Although I do not believe in a creator who would intentionally cause devastation, I do believe that we need to create a sense of reason and a renewed will to come out of our own darkness. This means looking to the highest good, even when we absolutely can't see it.

It has been imperative for me to see life as a series of events that led me to where I am today. That doesn't mean I have to like them, but only I can pull myself out of hell. So where are you today and what has led you to this book? Have you been on a quest for meaning? Are there some life events that deserve your examination and love? Have you ever had an aha moment long after the fact, when *not* getting what you desperately wanted suddenly made sense? Even if life has treated you terribly up to now, I promise that consciously choosing to acknowledge your pain and heal will sow the seeds for change. That doesn't mean that the pain will abate immediately, or that you will be living in a fantasy land where all is perfect, but you will have begun the process. And you might gain a renewed sense of order and reason out of the unreasonable.

As I got sober and embraced the healing journey, I began to recognize that I was afraid and that only I could do something about it. Once I'd identified the problem, I could no longer play the victim. I began asking myself many questions inspired by twelve-step and narrative therapies that I did my best to answer honestly. Afterward, I would write in my journal to see what came up.

Was I allowing the horror that I felt as a child to affect me as an adult? Was I drinking to mask the deeply ingrained fear that I wouldn't be able to protect a child? Was I worried that I would be too self-absorbed and temperamental to respond to the cries of a child? Were my fears pushing me away from my husband? I wasn't able to shed light on everything, but I was on my way to taking responsibility and moving in a positive direction.

The years when I was sick and tired of it all, desperately trying to get better, were hard. I searched relentlessly to find self-love, and the trip was jerky, with many fits and starts, like a bad carnival ride. I just couldn't keep it together. I wanted to push those questions away. I remember lying there in yoga class in what was supposed to be relaxation pose or savasana, retraumatized by my own physical sensations, afraid of my racing thoughts, and wanting to blame it on the "bad teacher" rather than taking the time to really look at what was going on inside me. This type of hypervigilance followed me everywhere. I came to learn that I was constantly scanning the environment for threats and, at the time, alcohol was the only thing that quelled it.

But as I started to clean up my life, my hands stopped shaking, and I stopped anticipating that glass of wine at four o'clock. Life was beginning to shift, and I began to realize that the power to change lay in my hands.

I want to point out that many of my own traumatic memories have been frozen in time or lost in a blackout. If this is your story, please don't fret. The Name Work in the next chapter can and will work for you if you let it. Somatic healing expert Dr. Peter Levine writes,

"We don't have to know the facts of our story to be able to reprogram the outcomes."

In the end, it becomes necessary for me to remind myself that life doesn't happen in a straight line. I'm bound to slip in one way or another. Although I'm currently following the direction of those in recovery and I don't drink or use no matter what, I continue to remind myself that the willingness to feel whatever troubles me makes my healing a possibility. When I allow myself to feel, I am ready to go deep into this powerful work. Although the darkness may seem like an eternity, there is always light at the end of the tunnel.

I've been on the sober path pretty much ever since meeting Ram Dass, one of my spiritual teachers, but I want to say here that not everyone will necessarily be supportive of your feelings or your grieving process. One day, after a group chant, a friend introduced me to the visiting singer/teacher and told him that my daughter had died just a few months earlier. He was someone I really looked up to. A leader. I expected him to offer me some words of wisdom as he stood there in front of a huge statue of Lord Shiva, the great change maker with many arms. He just stared at me blankly. Speechless. He didn't say a word until he began making small talk. "Hey, man," he said, "is that coffee shop open down the street?"

I was upset and disillusioned at the time, but I realized later that we have to let people off the hook. Some of them simply don't know what to say, whether they are spiritual leaders or not. Even worse, I have heard of spiritual leaders telling mourners that God doesn't want them to cry. If this is happening to you, run! We need to seek out situations and circumstances that will ultimately help us, and we need to find the courage to leave those that don't. I have found on this path that, when one person seemingly drops the ball and disappoints, there is another to better fill his or her shoes if I continue to seek help.

And then there was the eye-opening process of learning to become my own best friend, learning to sit alone in silence, aware of my breath. It is here that change really happened, the kind of change that comes from having the courage to get out of my own way and step onto the healing path.

As I "trudged this road" as many in my circle like to say, I learned that by treating myself kindly and staying sober, I could be a good wife and mother. This could never have happened without my conscious decision to heal. My past family mantras had been:

> "I hate myself and I want to die."
> "I'm a bad girl."
> "Everybody is laughing at me."
> "Get out the Doritos and eat the whole bag."
> "Stain the new sheets while you're at it, because life sucks and then you die."

I decided to begin the process of shedding those stale mantras. And, if I'm honest with myself, I'm still sloughing off the old gunk to this day. As they say, "progress, not perfection." What matters most is that I saw an antidote and people out there believed that I could stop the self-hating chatter in my mind. This was revolutionary. The reality that I could look within and lead a healthy life opened up a whole new world to me. I had a renewed sense of hope. For the first time, I truly believed that the desire to escape my pain through drink could be removed.

When I finally began working on change, it wasn't like watching a heavenly glitter ball drop. It was noisy and crowded in my head, and I didn't have a clear view of the marquee or the neon lights. The noise in my mind was too loud to take in the cheering. The party was happening, but somehow I was missing it. There was no angelic disco band and no streamers when the change happened—only a pinprick of love and light that made it through the darkness and noise. It was just a little ray. I still felt like a gnarly wart-faced creature, and I was desperate. But for the first time, I stopped blaming myself for the cesspool I was in. Instead of wallowing in it and feeling like crap, I took action.

I eventually learned that we have to be kind to ourselves and give ourselves love when we are in trauma, when we are the victim, or even when something is absolutely our fault. We have to be kind when there is nothing we can do to stop the shit show. The consequences are the consequences. We must begin where we are, even if we are literally behind bars.

I was in what they call the pink cloud of sobriety, alive with possibility. For the first time in my life, I felt like I was sane enough to have a baby, to truly commit to my husband, and to have a full family life. I was all lit up. My life had become a moving prayer. I practiced yoga, I chanted, I went to twelve-step meetings, and I embraced affirmative living and the idea of a loving God. I lost Kara when I was only a few years sober and on a solid path. Thank God for my sober sisters and spiritual support, without which I would not have survived. Along my journey, I met several women in the meeting who had also lost children. We all held each other tightly, and I knew that if I began drinking again, it would be the death of me.

"It comes in bloody waves," one of the women told me. I knew this. I knew that a wave of grief could knock me off my feet. But The Name Work steadied me and got me going again.

CHAPTER 5

Incubation

I created The Name Work out of a desire to make positive changes in the world and to share what I have learned in order to help others. After we lost Kara, I spent a lot of time in solitude. I knew I wanted to create a foundation in Kara's name, but I didn't know what it would look like. While my creative vision for The Name Work was incubating, I hiked the mountains just above our home.

I listened to the sound of my boots crunching against the gravel. Even my feet were praying for an answer. It was on these hikes that the letters in Kara's name became most vivid in my mind's eye. I saw how her name could become a road map to a better place.

While I was pondering The Name Work, I decided to host and donate to Kuumba, a camp for kids, founded by Rickie Byars, which was affiliated with Agape. I held a gathering in our backyard to help kids and give back to the Agape community that had helped me in my darkest hours. I didn't know it then, but this step forward planted the seed for the Kara Love Project, the foundation that I created in Kara's name.

It started in small quiet ways, partly because grieving had affected my lungs. I had chronic bronchitis and debilitating brain fog, so much so that it was difficult having simple conversations. I was in the worst shape of my life, and it seemed like I was sick all the time. I was down for the count, on antibiotics and inhalers just to breathe. But I kept hiking when I could, spending many hours in the mountains and on my yoga mat.

We held the kickoff for the Kara Love Project on a perfect October night. Our Westside community came out to support us as local kirtan artists chanted. We sang along, looking up to the heavens, and I told the story of Kara's brief life and how I wanted to raise money for the Unatti Home for Girls in Bhaktapur, Nepal, in her memory. The home was founded by a wonderful woman named Stephanie Waisler Rubin. I heard unfathomable stories of children, hungry and cold, eating off floors and sleeping on cement. I saw photos of the girls and read their names. I wanted to touch their lives in a profound way. Mere fundraising was not enough; I wanted to breathe more life and meaning into all my projects. I was through turning away from my suffering, stuffing it all down like a bag of popcorn. I wanted to become a more realized, conscious human being. And so I heeded the call of my soul and flew across the world to meet the girls myself.

Today, the Kara Love Project donates to a number of charitable causes and has created a Wellness Initiative for those in need. We provide workshops, restorative retreats, and therapeutic sessions to people of all ages. As an offshoot of the Kara Love Project, I created The Name Work, which is the subject of this book. The idea that the letters in each of our names hold mystical and holy value is not new. The ancient Kabbalists ascribed holy meaning to each letter of the Hebrew alphabet, and the letters are rich with metaphor. It is my contention that the letters and qualities we find within someone's name in our English language can also help us change and access deep spiritual states. The Name Work shows us how to go within to explore the qualities in the letters of our chosen names to create what is called "a field of infinite possibilities" and move through stuck life circumstances. My life is filled with a sense of purpose and renewal from creating and using the sacred grouping of qualities that I derived through working with Kara's name.

Working with the qualities you unearth through the letters is a good way to begin mapping out or setting an intention regarding what you want for your life. When we listen to the callings of our own soul, our names become road maps to reunite with our ever-present Higher Selves. Don't worry if you think your name is too long or too short or if you like another quality with a letter that is not in your name. Try not to fret if some of the qualities you find don't seem to apply. Just stay open and willing to work with what you've been given. Even if your name has an X in it, there are qualities for you to explore. There is Xenodochial, which means being friendly to strangers. Or Xenial, which means sharing hospitality between host and guest. The questions will guide you to see where you fit in relation to these qualities. If you don't have a name that resonates, you can try creating your own spiritual name with qualities that make sense to you. Or you can even find characteristics within a chosen quality to move you forward.

When I embrace the healing journey and see that pain is a part of the healing process, I can begin to create a more holistic vision of life. I want to say here that if I had continued to insist that God was punishing me by taking my baby or that my negative thinking caused it, I would have destroyed myself. Even in the seemingly endless depths of my pain, I had to act as if there was a loving God. My faith may have faltered during this time, but I don't buy for a second that my "unkempt consciousness" caused Kara to lose her breath and die. That said, it is very important to understand that being unwilling to shift my thoughts around her death would most certainly have killed me. Things can suck, but I can't allow them to suck me under. In order to practice The Name Work, I became willing to talk myself off the cliff with words of love. Even now, when the darkness lingers, I make use of the tools that at the very least keep me from jumping. To do this, I embrace the philosophy of "contrary action" to fill my consciousness with thoughts that conjure a greater sense of possibility and meaning.

When I was still shell-shocked with grief, I needed to go straight to affirmative statements. At first, I could only recite pieces of them. I needed to start slowly and seek support. The Buddhist philosophy emphasizes that we are all connected, and that to be human is to suffer. No matter how great your life or someone else's life looks, we all struggle in one way or another. It is what we choose to do with our suffering that defines us. All we need to do is look at some of the world's greatest teachers to see that we can reap great things out of the worst life circumstances.

I have embraced the idea that our scars can become our greatest blessings. There are countless wounded healers, teachers, and leaders who have made this world a better, more compassionate place. Abraham Lincoln lost a child and went on to become one of the greatest presidents of the United States. Mahatma Gandhi and Martin Luther King Jr. felt the sting of discrimination and hate, yet they sent messages of peace and nonviolence, inspiring millions. After a childhood of poverty and abuse, Oprah Winfrey uses her journey to lead people out of the darkness and toward the greater good. There was also one of my teachers, Ram Dass, who continued to teach for twenty years in a failing body after a massive stroke. He found a way to shine amidst adversity, showing us all the meaning of fierce grace. And last but not least, there is Jesus, the Savior for many, who was crucified for teaching his followers how to love one another, in spite of the pain in the world. These beautiful beings all went through tragedy and moved through it, helping others and shining light in the darkness.

In the spirit of these way-showers, The Name Work can and will enrich your life, if you are willing to take the journey within and embrace the process of self-discovery. When I asked myself the hard questions, I discovered where I'd been less than kind to myself in the grieving process. Through this work, I found that I was telling myself that I didn't deserve to be a mother and that I was somehow "cursed." Through getting quiet enough to listen to my inner chatter, I discovered that I continued to hold the thought that a vengeful God took my baby. This discovery helped me see it for what it was and turn away from that darkness. Without this work, this kind of inner dialogue would have destroyed my life.

Getting in touch with my pain helps me to plant new seeds in my consciousness and to stop uprooting the good with destructive self-talk. Today, I am able to affirm the following:

"I am a loving being who is attuned to her children."
"I am deserving of a beautiful family life."
"I nurture myself, my family, and all of my relationships."
"I deserve happiness."
"I am allowed to feel my feelings."
"I am a beautiful work in progress."

Through this work, I discovered where I'd been unkind. I also discovered when I was being kind in order to get what I wanted, rather than being kind for its own sake.

As you embark on The Name Work, I encourage you to find a support group or therapist to help guide you on this journey. Remember that this work is not linear. Godspeed.

PART II

"When I write, I pray, May what I put down here lift the Spirits of those who read it, give them hope and strength to meet what they have to meet, help them to keep faith and to find courage, help them above all to find meaning, for without meaning, what has any worth? To find meaning is to find God."

—James Dillet Freeman

CHAPTER 6

The Name Work

I had a vision when I decided to use my personal tragedy to heal myself. I was determined to make great changes. I was in Bhaktapur at the time; our car was bumping along the rutted roads as the dust swirled and the vivid colors of Nepal called out to me. That was where I found my purpose and when I decided to use the letters of Kara's name as my guide and assign special qualities to them. I also wanted to help others find healing and transformation through the letters in their own names or those of their loved ones.

The negative voice inside me told me that I couldn't create change that way. But a more receptive and compassionate voice urged me to play around with the idea. The concept was vague and amorphous at first, but my vision was coming into focus. When I returned home from Nepal, I remembered Reverend Michael Beckwith's wise words during my deepest despair: *The pain pushes until the vision pulls.*

I knew that my baby was here, and I had given her a name, so I asked myself, *What does Kara stand for?* I created a group of qualities from the letters in her name:

K is for Kindness:

Let's be kind to ourselves, to others, and to the environment.

A is for Alignment:

We focus our attention on what is good and right in the world, no matter how dark things may seem.

R is for Regeneration:

We commit to a practice that allows us to feel more spacious and puts us in touch with what we truly need.

A is for Action:

We do things that will help others along the way. That includes knowing when to be more engaged, when to slow down, and most importantly, to move toward Tikkun Olam, the healing of the world.

Activating the qualities in a name can change lives for the better when we take our insights out into the world. The question is, once you've chosen the name you want to break down, how do you find the corresponding qualities?

In order to give you ideas, I've included an A through Z Dictionary of Qualities at the back of this book that can assist you in moving through all kinds of challenges. Perhaps you're going through a divorce. The qualities that you're about to uncover in The Name Work will allow you to explore what is and what isn't working in your life. This is similar to what twelve-step programs call "taking a moral inventory." Delving into these qualities allows you to begin a process of rigorous self-questioning.

Let's say that a woman named Anette is going through a bitter divorce, and she wants to feel better. She begins by dissecting her own name, letter by letter, and finding qualities to work with. As she looks for an *A* word, the quality *Agreeable* jumps out at her. She notices that there is anything but Agreement in her life. She and her husband are in a horrific custody battle, and her bank accounts have been frozen. As the quality "agreeable" presents itself, it's a good sign, since it reminds her that it's beneficial to move through what causes her resistance or pain in order to come out the other side.

Let's explore how a quality that shows up can help us see and recognize where we can create necessary change. When Anette asks herself how the word *Agreeable* presents itself in her life, she can learn about her character traits. Then she begins to ask herself a set of specific questions in relation to that quality that beckons her to take the journey within:

1. Is there too much or too little Agreement in my life?
2. Are there times when having more of this quality would help?
3. How has this quality benefited me in the past?
4. Has it hurt me in the past? How?
5. Do I feel safe expressing Agreement in my life?
6. Have I ever been afraid of it?
7. How can I activate more Agreement?
8. How did Agreement show up for me as a child?
9. Has the opposite quality shown up in my life?

If you are anything like Anette and you begin to explore the *Agreeable* quality and honestly answer the above questions, you'll begin to see how few boundaries you had in place during your marriage. By being honest with yourself, you can see that perhaps you have been too agreeable. Anette realized that she had become a doormat in her marriage, catering to her narcissistic husband's every whim until she couldn't take it any longer. She realizes that she has a history of discomfort around saying no, out of a need to please others.

If you have a habit of people-pleasing, ultimately, you may need to learn to disagree. Agreeing to stay in an abusive relationship will only hurt you, so you need to be less than agreeable as you assert yourself. As you explore the word "agreeable," you can tap into your fear of creating discord and recognize that it's okay to disagree. In fact, you *need* to disagree for your own well-being. The surprising thing is that, when you get in touch with disagreeing, you will also find out what agrees with you.

After Anette works with the first letter, *A*, she moves on to *N*, and the quality *Newness* jumps out. She asks herself the same set of questions and realizes that she's afraid of the unknown—afraid of what's new.

She moves on to *E*, and *Emotional* comes up. She can see where she's out of touch with her emotions and how she is pushing them away.

There are two *T*s in her name. She chooses *Talented* and *Truthful*. She needs to find her talents, what she likes and doesn't like. She needs to find out what she's good at, and she sees that she needs to express more truthfulness and stand up for what she believes. This is how she finds her willingness to disagree.

The last letter is another *E*. She chooses *Energetic* because she feels a lack of energy in her life. She finds that she needs to allow for better nutrition and sleep. She also discovers that she is secretly afraid of being too energetic.

Like Anette, exploring all of the above qualities will allow you to evaluate what is working and what isn't. Are you subconsciously afraid of disagreeing? By moving toward the resistance and discomfort, you can find a way to create change.

As a child, I didn't feel safe speaking up for my wants and needs. But when I think about the quality *Agreeable* and and how it manifests in my life, I can activate the changes I want. I can also change my thinking in relation to the qualities I discover.

After you've decided what quality you need to work on, you can begin the process of positively affirming what you want. Here are some sample affirmations (positive messages) based on the inherent qualities in the word *Anette*.

1. I live in Agreement with my own life. I establish healthy boundaries. I recognize that "No" is a complete sentence, that it's okay to say no if something makes me uncomfortable. I don't need to justify it.

2. I embrace newness and invite new opportunities into my life.

3. I recognize, feel, and move through my emotions in order to create positive change.

4. I explore my unique talents and move toward that which is joyful.

5. I discover, uncover, embrace, and live by my truth.

6. I get more energy by getting proper sleep and eating foods that sustain me.

Working with the various qualities sheds light on areas in our lives that need our love and attention. Reverend Michael Beckwith teaches that we manifest where we pay the most attention. He often says, "Energy flows where attention goes." If I focus on what is wrong, I will bring more of that into my experience. He is not preaching that my thinking is what caused Kara to die, or what put our friend Anette in an awful divorce. Yet it is only me and my willingness to shift focus and perspective that can lead me out of the darkness. Having this willingness also allows me to seek the help of qualified teachers, therapists, peers, or guides. Even though I have to answer to myself, I can also seek out community.

When I was taking coursework at the Agape Spiritual Center, we were advised to enunciate and make our affirmative statements sound like we truly believed them. As hundreds of us held hands on Sundays and Wednesdays amidst vibrant hues of purple, pink, orange, and green, we did just that. I was wrapped in the power of the collective blanket. We were there to heal, a critical and prayerful mass who were engaged and ready, surrounded by artful renderings of mentors and way-showers like Mother Teresa, Martin Luther King, Jesus, and Mahatma Gandhi.

We made our affirmations in a simple sanctuary, which at the time was a warehouse in an office park. We were there to see the best in each other as we jumped, shouted joyfully, and prayed out loud. I still have an inspirational memento that Reverend Michael gave us during one particular ceremony: a heart-shaped crystal the size of a nickel. It was a few short months after Kara died, and there we stood in a line that wound around the sanctuary, waiting for our gift like we would have waited to take a communion wafer. The music of Rickie Byars filled the air.

"I pray that you will see the best of life, the best of love, the very best of everything."

I wept with hopelessness amidst the divine energy as I received my crystal and held onto my vision. We ate at a greasy-spoon diner afterward and I pretended to enjoy the company of friends. I knew then that life moves on with or without us. In this "be here now" moment of clarity, I knew that Michael was right, that professing our affirmations with vision and determination is the best way to proceed.

Within this larger, all-pervasive context of goodness and vision, The Name Work encourages each of us to explore our lives. The beautiful and challenging part of this work is that, when we explore the qualities in the letters of our names, we can discover parts of ourselves that we don't normally see. Perhaps I've been hanging out with the same five or six people since high school. Maybe I've spent time with a few coworkers and I haven't given myself the chance to meet new people.

Isn't it time to take that art class with a room full of strangers? I've been dreaming about that for years and now that my kids are driving, I have free time on Saturdays. Why not get more creative with my life as I follow the qualities in a name? Taking ourselves out of our comfort zones will lead us into positive action.

When you're doing The Name Work, here are a few things to ask yourself. We have already detailed some of these questions using Anette's example, but they are worth repeating. How does each quality present itself in my life? Is there too much or too little of it? Is there just enough? How can I express more of it? Am I comfortable with it, or not so much? How has this quality benefited me in the past? How can it benefit me in the future? Have I ever been afraid of it? Has it ever negatively impacted me? Have I demonstrated the opposite of this quality? What can I learn about myself through examining it? How did my parents demonstrate this quality? Was it present in my childhood? Is it present today in my intimate relationships and friendships?

If these questions are overwhelming, you can come back to them later. Please note that feeling the gamut of seemingly negative emotions is crucial and that being in a state of overwhelm can be a catalyst for healing. In the same breath, it is also important to remember that simply knowing I have grief or trauma and what caused it is useless, unless I treat myself with kindness and love. To be clear, an awareness of the emotional bumps and bruises that I got during my formative years does not necessarily challenge me to create a more loving and positive narrative. Through practicing The Name Work, I learned to make space for uncomfortable feelings and bodily sensations, and, at the same time, I used the self-soothing method of repeating gentle affirmations. Without pushing away discomfort, the use of gentle affirmations gives me the ability to create positive change from the inside out. I may not feel the change immediately, but over time things can and will change for the better. Self-Discovery and Self-Love are at the core of The Name Work. It is a positive practice of a number of different modalities such as positivity, movement, meditation, and breath work that make healing more accessible.

If you are ready to experiment with affirmations and see how they feel, I urge you to stop and take three full and deep conscious breaths. After you have taken a pause, go to the back of the book and read through the A through Z Dictionary. Choose several qualities and sample affirmations to use on a daily basis. Or you can use the qualities I found in the name Kara.

CHAPTER 7

Affirmations and Prayers

According to Ernest Holmes, founder of the Science of Mind philosophy, if we change our thinking, we can change our lives. One of the ways we can do this is to use affirmations to change our thought patterns. So far, we've explored the power of thought by using our friend Anette as an example. But what exactly is an affirmation? It is a positive statement we make about our environment and ourselves. Using affirmations can help us move through the darkness and into a more grounded and centered space.

I use affirmations in every aspect of the Kara Inspired Grouping of Qualities. They are the bedrock of the Kara meditations and are woven into the tapestry of my life in good times and in bad. They help me activate Kindness toward myself and others. They help me see the importance of Universal Alignment, reminding me to take time to pause and regenerate. Finally, they help me when I'm in action, living my day-to-day life. I'm grateful to my teachers for giving me this concrete method to usher in positive and light-filled feelings.

One of my first experiences with affirmative thinking was at the Unity Church in Kansas City with Reverend Duke Tufty. Although I still had many mountains to climb, he taught me about the importance of having a personal relationship with God or a Higher Power. His teaching was revolutionary. In order to have a relationship with a Higher Power, he told me that I needed to love myself. In fact, he went a step further and taught me that I *was* love, that God is love. Through his Cornerstone Foundation, he brought cutting-edge speakers to his center. I was able to listen to revolutionary thinkers like Judith Orloff, Marianne Williamson, and others who taught me that God, intuition, or the Holy Spirit within me had the power to lead me out of the darkness.

This was all mind-blowing to a young woman who suffered and replayed the gamut of negative emotions. As I mentioned earlier, I come from a long line of people who were good at practicing the art of self-hatred. "I hate myself and want to die" was a popular mantra. I began to try something else. I began what Father Leo Booth calls "transforming my God Box." That means I began to make affirmations and reassess what God and Life meant to me. I gave myself permission to explore.

I remember my first time walking into that Unity Temple. The musty, lemony smell reminded me of my youth at my family synagogue. It felt like a good place to find God. A beautiful stained-glass work of art with a picture of the bible hung over the altar. The word *LOVE* was written on the glass, surrounded by beautiful hues of pink, purple, yellow, and green. I felt safe there.

I remember sitting in Reverend Tufty's office one day, sobbing. I gazed down at my sunny yellow Benetton sweater. "I don't know what I'm going to do with my life. Nothing is working and I'm so anxious, I can't even drive my car." I ranted on and on, working myself into a state of panic. He listened for a long time, encouraged me to keep coming to the temple, and he handed me a book of affirmations. Today, I smile when I think of his beautiful temple, and I am reminded to understand the powerful role that my mind plays in making my life a heaven or a hell. When I'm in fear, I put the Unity principles into practice. One of my favorite prayers that I committed to memory was the "Prayer for Protection," by James Dillet Freeman. It is like a beacon of light.

It reads:

> *The light of God surrounds me;*
> *The love of God enfolds me;*
> *The power of God protects me;*
> *The presence of God watches over me;*
> *Wherever I am God is!*

Those beginning moments at Unity were beautiful. The idea that there was a loving God moving in, around, and through me gave me a great deal of comfort and ignited a life-changing process within me. We lived in Kansas City for a few short years, and when we moved, Reverend Tufty directed me to Reverend Michael and his wife, Rickie, who ran the Agape choir. When Kara passed away, I was thankful that I'd been pointed in their direction. I had been going there for a few years before Kara died, feeling blessed to have found a sanctuary in our chaotic city. When it happened, I reached out and called Rickie.

"She's dead, Rickie," I said through my sobs.

She suggested I start singing with the choir. "You already know all the songs," she said encouragingly.

I took her advice. I remembered the twelve-step instruction to "act as if." I told myself to act as if and it would come. I told myself to believe there was light at the end of the tunnel, even though I couldn't see it. And in that darkness, I reached out in kindness to myself. I sang for a few months dressed in bright white, purple, and other glowing colors. I felt like ash. But, thankfully, I was a few years sober and without a nagging hangover. In divine time, I would allow my breath, unobstructed by chemicals, to become an invisible healing force, a moving prayer.

Affirmations helped me both before and after Kara's death, as they offered a positive way to work with difficult emotions. I had to learn to face my anger and sadness, and, later, my grief, in order to move through it. In order to heal, I had to slow down and learn to breathe as I repeated affirmations that sounded silly at first.

I am loved. I am safe. I am protected. I am love. God is love.

There are a few things I learned about creating affirmations back then. If I am in a dark place, I need to become good at conjuring up positivity. I need to look at what is good and right in the world. I can use my senses to do this. What have I seen with my eyes that I know for sure I can love? Back then, I knew for sure that I loved my neighbor's basset hound, Molly. I loved her long floppy ears and rubbing her tummy. What could I hear that offered me comfort? I loved the songs of James Taylor. And taste and smell? I loved my grandmother's cooking and the scent of the beautiful flowers in her back yard.

When I list these things that I can feel with my five senses, I am more readily able to come into a positive space. If I was in a dark space, feeling like there was no love in the world, all I would need to do was picture that sweet dog, Molly. I've briefly mentioned that an important aspect of affirmative statements is that we need to say them like we mean them. In other words, we need to "fake it till we make it." When I found myself repeating that horrible mantra, "I hate myself," picturing Molly helped me turn it around. I would say "I love myself" with conviction.

In order to create affirmations, I spoke a quality aloud and watched what came up in my mind. This gave me a good way to evaluate what was happening and to decide what I wanted to call into my life. For example, if the word was *affection*, I looked to see where affection was present and absent in my life, both past and present. Then I wrote about what I wanted to see more of or "manifest" in my life. I also remembered to avoid the word *not*. For example, if I want to have a better relationship with my husband, it's a bad idea to affirm "Don't fight with your husband." Remember to avoid *don't*, *not*, and *can't* when you're making affirmative statements. You want to construct an affirmation as if it is already done. For example, if I tend to be cold and not affectionate, I construct an affirmation which "acts as if" I am already affectionate.

Here are some examples of affirmations for the quality of Affection:

- I show affection to my children and they show affection toward me. The affection I give is multiplied.
- I am worthy of affection. I treat myself with kindness and affection every day by taking time for myself.
- I take time to give my husband affection, and our intimate relationship is enhanced as a result of the love I give.
- I find constructive ways to love myself.

I learned that affirmations were not meant to be harsh orders to myself. They were visionary statements that activated the life I wanted to live in my conscious mind. I breathed in loving myself. I breathed out loving others. I took the words of Reverend Michael and reminded myself that the Universe was *for* me, not *against* me. This became my mantra as I began to enjoy exercising my body. I kept saying the affirmation *I love my body*, even when I was filled with doubt, putting one foot in front of the other and acting as if it was already happening.

CHAPTER 8

K Is for Kindness

When I lay in the hospital waiting for Kara to be born, my friend Micheline brought me an orchid plant. It felt like its magenta leaves were filled with hope. In hindsight, the plant kept me alive and hopeful during those humdrum hospital days. The last bud came into full bloom on the day my daughter was born.

When it was time to leave the hospital and go home, I was hobbling from the C-section, wincing in pain, when I called to David, "Don't forget the orchid plant." He and I both felt connected to it, so we carefully transported it with our baby in her car seat for her very first ride. Once we got home, I placed that beautiful plant in our kitchen. It was thriving—until the day Kara left us. When she died, that plant shriveled too, as its once-majestic flowers crumbled in the dirt. The orchid was evidence that we are all more connected to the earth then we think. At the time, I couldn't see it. I was too devastated and angry. But that same force kept me going.

I clung to the advice Reverend Michael gave me when I first lost Kara. "You can grow or shrink from this tragedy," he said. I knew what I had to do, and I sought help. As I sat on my purple mat on the floor of my yoga studio and looked up at the ceiling fan, I listened to a kirtan musician chant the many sacred names of God. People were dancing; they seemed to be moving in slow motion, and it was unbearable. I was near-catatonic and the dancing and drumbeats made no sense to me. I wanted to fade away like a name in the sand. I went home depleted and more depressed than when I came. What I didn't know at the time was that these acts of self-care were planting seeds. Soon, a renewal would happen, and I would bloom once again.

I realized that kindness to myself meant having the willingness to begin again. I had a spiritual mentor and therapist, Marilyn, who said, "Keep your car on the road and keep moving." She told me that kindness to self meant rising out of the darkness and facing the day, no matter how difficult it might seem. I gave myself permission to distance myself from people who weren't helpful and to move closer to those who were.

Kindness is a practice. I continue to learn and re-learn what kindness to self looks like so that I can show up for life. I believe that if I hadn't first learned to be kind to myself, Kara would not have come to this earth. And in being kind to myself as I moved through pain and suffering, I became more readily able to be kind to others. In 12 Step, reaching out to others is what helps us get unstuck in our own pain and suffering. I remember a quote that I pinned on my bulletin board by Thomas Mann that gives hope. It reads: "Only people who suffer can be a guide and healer to those who are suffering."

My yoga teacher, Mark, was a great help to me. The foundation of yoga is breathing, but in the aftermath of my loss, I told my teacher that I didn't want to breathe. He didn't try to fix me, but gradually I went back to my breathing practice in my own time. As I began to breathe again, I realized that kindness to self meant there was no more judging the part of me that wanted to say fuck it all to hell and throw in the towel. I needed to allow myself the space to grieve. It also meant accepting help and listening to friends who were wise and loving.

"Don't give up," they told me. "You'll have more babies."

"What about the baby I just lost?" I moaned. Still, I recited the mantra "I will have more babies."

In order to come to terms with my pain and suffering, I had to acknowledge that I wasn't the only one who was fucked up and insecure and in loads of pain. I wasn't the only one who felt misunderstood. I related to a meme on Facebook: "Everyone you meet is fighting a battle you know nothing about. Be kind. Always."

We never know what people are going through or what struggles they're facing. In twelve-step programs, we talk about "being of service." That might mean showing up for my child's dance class when I'd rather be at the gym or writing. It might mean letting my husband choose what we're watching on TV. It definitely means reading bedtime stories, scheduling play dates, and showing up with a smile. It also means becoming curious and taking an interest when I'm tired or I don't really have one.

If I hadn't created The Name Work, I might have stayed stuck. But when I took apart the qualities I found in Kara's name, I discovered what I needed to do. For me, working with organizations like the Unatti Foundation in Nepal was about kindness and service to others. It was beautiful to make the trek there and see what doing this work can accomplish. Exploring the quality of kindness showed me how much I wanted to help these girls and give them the opportunity of an education. As we came together to benefit Unatti, we made our vision a reality. Since then we have hand-picked a variety of organizations, Unatti included, for which we raised funds.

Being of service, however, doesn't mean that I stop caring for and being kind to myself. It means that I know myself well enough to be able to balance self-care with care for others. It requires taking time to be quiet each day. Doing a movement and breath practice like yoga has helped me a great deal. Simply listening to my breath every day brings me huge benefits. The late Harvard professor and LSD guru Timothy Leary said that we can all benefit from turning on, tuning in, and dropping out. He was talking about taking LSD, but we don't need psychotropic drugs to accomplish this.

It takes only a few moments. You might want to try it. On the inhale, move your hands upward to reach over your head. On the exhale, bring your hands back to your sides. Do it ten times and see what happens. When you commit to these kinds of simple practices, you'll feel better, smarter, wiser, and more connected. The truth is that we have a storehouse of chemicals and wisdom inside of us, just waiting to assist us in our healing. When I recognize instances when I was less than kind, I try to forgive myself. We can only be our best. The good news is that each moment is new, and we can always start over.

There are many ways to embrace kindness. You don't have to start a nonprofit to be kind. Small acts of kindness have a ripple effect. How about taking a moment to feed someone's parking meter that's about to expire? You don't have to dress up in a pair of pink wings like the parking fairy and make a scene. You can do it anonymously. You can let someone go ahead of you in the checkout line. You can be kind to the grouchy checkout clerk or the teenager with a dozen red hoop earrings standing in front of you. Or the guy at the deli counter who seems to be taking forever to fill your order. You don't have to sneer. Who knows what he's been through or why he has food stuck in his beard?

My rabbi, Neil Comess Daniels, says that we should never pass a homeless person on the street without offering a little something. I can't say that I follow his rule of thumb all the time, but I've gotten better. When I see the guy in need in the supermarket parking lot, I give him a bottle of fresh water and a few dollars every now and then. What does it take to purchase a floral arrangement or a dozen oranges from the guy at the crosswalk? Some of my best bouquets were purchased in a traffic jam from a nice man with a small daughter.

Along with kindness to self and others, we can't leave out kindness to the environment that is suffering from abuse and neglect. We are more connected to the earth than we know, but it took me a while to recognize this. Today, I wouldn't hurt a fly, but as a teenager, I used to smoke cigarettes, callously burning ants with my yellow Bic lighter, charring my lungs on the brick patio of our family home. *The ants are in my way,* I told myself. Even if they weren't, though, it wouldn't have mattered. I didn't have much respect for life back then, much less an army of ants.

I'm happy to say that, today, my life is radically different. I appreciate all living things, even ants. I am primarily a vegetarian and an aspiring vegan because I loathe the idea of pigs in gestation crates, unable to turn around for their entire lives. Or chickens being beefed up with so many hormones, they're unable to walk. I've seen way too many YouTube videos from the Humane Society of factory-farmed animals being kicked like footballs. This is hard to believe since I used to be a corn-fed Ho-Ho-eating youngster who loved going to Denny's for double cheeseburgers with my grandmother, taking shots of cream in little plastic cups and laughing.

Now, those delinquent days of tossing cigarette butts into the street are over. I eat well, I recycle, I turn the water off when I brush my teeth, and I do my best to be a good citizen. I'm no Mother Teresa, but I'm trying, and I can see that my healing and transformation have broadened my sensitivity to the environment, something that never would have happened if I hadn't gotten out of my own mucky mind, become vulnerable, and listened.

Kindness to self and the environment requires taking the time to get out in nature or even caring for a small house plant. Hiking taught me that the earth has a pulse, just like we do. If we want to live in sync with Mother Earth, we can start by defending her resources. Our lives become richer, deeper, and more fecund when we stop for a moment to feel our connectedness with our Mother.

I remember a time when I was on retreat, stretched out face down on the green lawn, listening to the hummingbirds at their feeders. The grass was tickling my cheek as I entertained the possibility of a more cosmic connection that I had only dreamt of. In recalling that moment, I can see that we all need to live on the earth in harmony. When the earth's water becomes polluted, we become sick with things like cancer. Just like we need to keep our bodies clean, we need to keep the earth clean. Granted, knowing this was different from living it. The moment of awareness was fleeting, but I was beginning to sprout. I began to understand that the earth's resources are like mother's milk, and I wanted to behave more like a dove than a tick. Bloodsucking and burning, the polar opposite of kindness, cannot bring me or anyone else happiness.

Kindness can exist in the most unexpected places. During times of trouble, I encourage you to persevere and be as kind to yourself as possible. As you experiment with loving kindness, some friends, teachers, and institutions will disappoint. Others will lift you up. You just need to keep trying until you find what works. Then you have to find the willingness to lift yourself up in spite of it all, taking support where it is offered. It may be a twelve-step group, a church, a synagogue, or a kirtan/yoga class. Just keep reaching for the positive. Even when someone lets you down, you can rise up by being kind and loving yourself. At this point, kindness to self means that I willingly expand my realm of possibilities without demanding a particular outcome.

Kara came into this world when I was sober and ready to be kinder to my body and soul. Why she left is still a mystery, but in that unspeakable grief, I needed to keep the door to kindness open. What I have learned is that kindness to self is not giving up when we are dealt seemingly horrific hands. Rather, it's about having the courage to incubate in the darkness, to emerge triumphantly, and to bring our work into the world. In the end, we learn to be kind to others when we practice the art of self-love. Here are some affirmations for kindness:

- I treat myself with loving kindness.
- I am worthy.
- I treat my body with kindness by eating healthy foods that nourish body and soul.
- I'm good enough.
- I'm kind to others of all ages and backgrounds.
- I look for kind qualities in others and the world.
- My friendships and relationships challenge me to grow.
- I choose to see good in the world.
- I am kind to the environment, and I honor the earth's resources.
- When I inhale, I think about being kind to myself. When I exhale, I think about being kind to others.
- The kindness I live is the kindness I give.
- The kindness of God surrounds me.

Here are some questions to ask yourself about kindness:

- How can I be kinder to myself? To others? The environment? List three ways you can increase the level of kindness in your life.

- How and where have I been the opposite of kind, or unkind? Do I need to "make amends" as they say in twelve-step programs?

- When has someone been unkind to me? Did I play a part in it?

- Was my mother kind to me? My father? Siblings? What messages did they give me regarding kindness?

- How can I take kindness out into my community and the world?

CHAPTER 9

A Is for Alignment

Metaphysical communities believe that each of us can make our lives a living heaven or a living hell. If you move away from alignment and goodness, you are in hell. If you move toward alignment and what is good in the world, you are in heaven. Some say that the opposite of fear is faith. When we have faith, we believe that the stop lights will turn from red to green, the traffic will move, and somehow we will get to work on time. The late Viktor Frankl, psychiatrist, author, and Holocaust survivor, told us that in the death camps, prisoners found a way to grow plants, to play games, and they even laughed sometimes. It was their way of staying aligned.

When I am feeling less than human and the world seems like a gigantic bloodsucking tick, it helps me to write down a list of what is working in my life. I make sure to find at least five things, even if they're as basic as:

> My house slippers are comfortable.
> I have a nice bed to sleep in.
> I have a few hours to write.
> I haven't caught a cold this season.
> My life is filled with art and love.

If I can't find the words to summon gratitude, chanting kirtan and practicing yoga help me immensely. I do a little of this work daily because my spiritual practice is about having faith and being in alignment with myself, other people, and the world at large.

Now that my husband and I have two beautiful daughters, I hope they will always stay aligned to the Divine Mother/Father/God and the Universe as they grow into adulthood. I want life to be kind to them. When it knocks them down, I hope they can find faith in their alignment with the Universe. I want them to be able to conjure a sense of hope, a sense that all is well.

To help my girls foster a feeling of alignment and reverence for life, I created a butterfly hatchery with them that I learned about from my friends at the local Waldorf School. I ordered a kit from Insectlore. com and together we watched the caterpillars grow and change. They started off so small, if I didn't know they were there, I might have swept them up without a second thought. They looked like wet mud that I might scrape off the bottom of my shoe, and then whammy, drumroll...they grew into hairy centipede-like creatures with the ability to construct a cocoon or chrysalis around themselves. The process is revelatory and totally out of anyone's control.

When I began this project, I was a wreck over the caterpillars. I paced like a nervous dad waiting for a baby to be born. *Surely these cocoons aren't going to make it,* I thought to myself, obsessively checking the netted habitat the kit provided. The fruit gunk they were eating didn't seem like enough. *The conditions aren't right*, I thought. My hemming, hawing, and relentless pacing proved to be for naught. One day, when I forgot for a moment, when I wasn't looking, the chrysalises began to transform into butterflies.

"Mommy, come see!" my seven-year-old called out to me. "A butterfly is here!"

We walked down the hall to the hatchery and lo and behold! A butterfly had arrived. It had happened out of my control. All I did was provide the right conditions. I marveled that the process had taken about a month, and then it happened in a snap. In fact, after the first butterfly was born, the entire butterfly community appeared fast, like microwave popcorn.

They had evolved, leaving behind their shells, which were dry and empty. They got to live butterfly lives independent of my obsessive worrying, all except for one that stayed stuck in limbo. It never completely shed its caterpillar cocoon, while the other butterflies were strong. The poor little guy was lugging around half of his cocoon and he lay withered and damp, bleeding red, his monarch-colored wings looking like wet tissue paper.

There was nothing I could do. Why did one caterpillar never get to enjoy a stint as a butterfly? He was given the same conditions as the others. He had the same shot at life. Had I handled the butterfly cage too roughly? Had my black cat, Wonka, scared him when she discovered the location and playfully swatted at the habitat? The what-ifs and shoulda-woulda-couldas began to swirl in my mind. Why was that poor little butterfly never meant to spread its wings? Maybe he was just passing through. We gave it our best shot, and I realized it was pointless to ruminate over the one butterfly that didn't make it. I was able to glimpse the bigger picture.

Just like that butterfly, our precious Kara wasn't meant to have a full human experience. And I have to continue on. I may not like the hand I've been dealt, but when I understand that there is a bigger picture, a Universal Alignment that exists regardless of my obsessive worrying, I can find some peace. When I take the time to breathe and stretch, when I allow myself to slow down and feel the magical alignment in the world around me, I can see a bigger picture. So much is out of my control and my responsibility is to create the kindest, most peaceful environment I can. In this moment, I am at peace with my alignment, with the universal blueprint that I can't see.

These days, no matter how dark it gets, I need to affirm that there is Universal Alignment in this world as I turn my attention to what is good and right.

Here are some affirmations about Alignment:

- I affirm Universal Alignment. God is working for my good.
- I step into alignment with my healthy lifestyle.
- Although I may not see it, everything is happening according to Universal Alignment.
- Everything is in divine order.

I recommend that you write in a journal and ask yourself the following questions about Alignment:

- What feels out of alignment in my personal, professional, and spiritual life?
- Do I believe that Universal Alignment and God are good?
- When I'm facing grief or obstacles, how can I "act as if" the Universe is aligned, that goodness and order exist?
- How have I experienced Universal Alignment in my life? Are there coincidences and aha moments that I can remember?
- What did my early religious upbringing teach me about God and alignment?

CHAPTER 10

R Is for Regeneration

When Kara died, David and I let everything go. I ate enough for two, David stopped shaving for nearly a year, and we let our yard grow wild. It wasn't like we consciously let it go. We were just somewhere else, having temporarily left behind the land of the living. The only place I went was to my weekly twelve-step group and sometimes out with my sobriety sisters and a few trusted friends.

A year had passed when I realized that our yard looked like a dilapidated scene out of *Grey Gardens*. I can't say what provoked this awakening, but I suddenly saw how bad it had gotten. I stood outside in my pink bathrobe and screamed, "Oh my God, David, look! We've killed our trees! We've killed them!"

The grass was swallowing our house, the ivy was overgrown, and the trees were heavy and untrimmed, providing a haven for rats and coyotes. A concrete angel who had lost a wing lay toppled in the dirt. Our sprinkler system was turned the wrong way and water was literally rotting out the trunks of two very large trees. I was so out of it, all I had to do was start wearing skirts on my head and they just might cart me off!

David and I surveyed the disaster that was our yard. The bottoms of two of the tree trunks were messed up in a big way. Maybe the dark thick scabs on their trunks were enough to yank us back into life. We put our heads together, we called the arborist, and we began to get things right again.

It took nearly seven years for all the trees to recover. To this day, the bottom of one of the trees looks like someone took a machete to it. It was barren for a few seasons while the other trees were thriving. After we spent a fortune on vitamin shots, I could see a few tiny bits of green on the straggler. We wondered if it would ever really grow back when I read a book about a woman who talked to trees in Findhorn, Scotland. I started talking to the tree. "I'm sorry I forgot about you, Tree. I was in my own sadness and grief. I didn't think about you, and I'm sorry."

One day, the tree began to bloom with yellow flowers. I didn't remember it ever growing flowers before. It felt like a miracle. As I watched the trees coming back to life, I realized that healing and regeneration don't happen overnight. The tree's seven-year journey taught me that I needed to give myself time. I needed to get down on my knees on my yoga mat and pray.

I wrote in my journal, practiced yoga daily, took bubble baths, and hiked in the mountains above our home. I did whatever activities helped me regenerate and brought me a sense of peace. During that time, I utilized a breathing exercise that worked for me. Maybe it will work for you, too. I invite you to put down your book and take three deep, slow, conscious breaths, in through the nose and out through the nose. Now do the same thing, inhaling with your arms over your head. Exhale and bring your arms down to your sides. Continue with these motions as you inhale, pause, as you exhale, pause. Do you see how this allows you to check in with yourself? To feel what is going on inside you? Repeat this three times and then lie down on your back and rest with your feet up on a chair. This is just a mini-suggestion, but why not do it for a while and see how it makes you feel?

I understood when I began to breathe deeply that, if I wanted to live life to its fullest, I had to find a way to pause and regenerate.

We all want to do that, but it looks different for everyone. We are all individuals and we have our own personal thumbprints. That means we have to find what works best for us. For me, restorative yoga came first and everything else followed. If I was feeling particularly ill at ease and I had extra time, I did some breathing and I listened to a self-healing CD. The most important thing is not to torture yourself over whether or not you're doing it right. Just start doing it! There is no right or wrong.

As David and I took back our yard and our lives, we fixed the fallen angel. She had lain in the dirt for a few seasons and now, when I look closely at her concrete wings, I can see where she has been mended. Similar to the orchid plant that died alongside our precious girl, I believe that the angel lost her wings when I fell into the depths of despair. It took me a long time to get the wherewithal to fix her. Today, when I look at her cement scars, I feel an almost visceral connection. I once was as broken as she was. Now, she and I are both intact. And, although some days look better than others, I can move and breathe again.

Regenerating daily is actually a major part of your action plan. This is how you stop yourself from fizzling out. Once you find that space inside you that is calm, centered, and peaceful, it is from this centered place that you get to the juicy center of things. You can see that there is nothing to fix, so you can spend your time thinking of areas in which you would like to grow and create change.

Keep in mind that we can't expedite our regeneration. It happens in its own time when we step back and let it all go. Just like our yard and the fallen angel, our scars can become our greatest blessings when we allow them to push us deeper into the ocean of healing.

As Reverend Rickie Byars so eloquently sings, "The seed needs the darkness to change into new life." If we can just hang on through the dark times, change will come.

Affirmations for Regeneration:

- Each day I take time to pause and regenerate.
- My body is my temple. I treat it as such, giving myself the ability to regenerate.
- The cells in my body regenerate. I am healthy, whole, and my life is complete.
- My body is in alignment with Spirit and I am pure health.
- I regenerate by finding new ways to care for myself.
- I eagerly try new healing modalities.
- I move into wholeness.
- I move into stillness.
- Breathing in, I am peaceful. Breathing out, I emanate peace.
- I create a sacred space in my home that feels good to me.

Questions to ask yourself about Regeneration:

- What are the ways I find to rest? How is my overall health?
- What is my diet like? Is there anything I want to change?
- Do I use alcohol or drugs to "take the edge off?" Would I like to change this?
- How much time do I spend watching TV? How about being on social media? Am I willing to try out new ways to spend my free time?
- What healing modalities am I willing to try?
- How often do I exercise? What does fitness look like? Am I kind to myself while I'm exercising?

- Do I send myself kind messages and repeat kind affirmations?

- Is my work commute a long one? Are there regenerative practices I can use when I'm traveling?

- Where can I create a sacred space for myself? Do I find time to take ten deep and slow breaths? Am I comfortable with silence?

CHAPTER 11

A Is for Action

My life was in chaos when I decided to create a plan of action from a centered place. Intuition doesn't come when our thoughts are racing. When we slow down, however, we can move forward in more positive and constructive ways. Taking action involves making space for regeneration as well as creating healthy boundaries.

If your boundaries are too rigid, you're not going to allow anyone to help you and your life will become constricted. I deny myself opportunities when no is my default answer. The garden-variety example of rigidity is a person who grows up with one or two overbearing parents who are way too involved in his or her business. They offer no personal space or autonomy as they eavesdrop on phone calls, read private journals, and barge into the bathroom or bedroom unannounced. The child grows up believing that everyone will violate her personal space, so she becomes a loner. But she also craves the company of people.

When we are facing a host of human problems such as addiction, loss, or a major life transition, fighting our own rigidity or "self-will" is essential. To truly feel the power of The Name Work, I needed to take myself out of self-imposed isolation and separateness. I had to remind myself that I didn't need to fall into "group think" or make sure everyone liked me to be a part of a group. And I needed to "keep coming back," even when I didn't want to. Having a plan for healing is a big part of my action plan. Being accountable to my weekly twelve-step group has been a huge part of my recovery from addiction and loss. My willingness to participate gave me the ability to work through a myriad of emotions within the stability of a group.

If your boundaries are too porous, you will probably spread yourself too thin. Perhaps you spent your childhood trying to please overly critical parents and could never do anything right in their eyes. As an adult, you might marry a man similar to your father and repeat the cycle of trying to please. You become a slave to your husband's needs and desires at the expense of your own. For example, you give up painting because your husband doesn't like the mess in the garage where he keeps his ever-growing power tool collection. You may become a doormat and end up feeling put upon and resenting others for their successes. There are a million projects that you want to get done, but you're so busy pleasing everyone else, you don't find the time to do what really fulfills you.

I know I'm spread too thin if I can't find time for stillness. That includes yoga, affirmations, and writing, which are at the core of The Name Work. As a mother, it's easy to get lost in my children's activities and planning for them becomes confused with "self-care." It's easy for me to disappear in this place, to forget about the affirmative process and unconsciously reach for a bag of pretzels when I've just had a nourishing dinner. When this happens, I need to remind myself that I can't possibly be a friend to others if I don't take care of myself. Sometimes, setting the kids up on their iPads or asking a friend to watch them while I do my practice is self-care. I know more than a few moms who trade nights so they can have some much-needed sacred time. What is the call of your soul? What do you do to nourish it?

Most of us fall somewhere in the middle of rigid and porous when it comes to receiving help and creating an action plan. If you're anything like me, you have extreme examples of too much and not enough.

When you're ready to move into the fourth quality, Action, remember not to move too fast, and that "No" is a complete sentence. It is helpful to ask yourself if the no is coming from a place of rigidity and fear. Or is the no putting healthy boundaries into place? Are you saying yes to please another person to your detriment? Or are you truly being of service?

When you become conscious about taking action, you show up for life in a constructive way that will benefit you. You learn to discern when to be with others and when to take time for yourself. If you don't take time to check in with yourself regarding when to move ahead and when to stay put and regenerate, you'll be spinning out and burning rubber.

I believe that working with the letters in our names or the names of our loved ones offers us a chance to look within and find out what we need and where we really want to go. This process affords us time to sense where we need to slow down and when we should move with more laser-focused action. Even if you feel pretty good and balanced about where you are, this process can take you on an exciting new journey if you're willing to do the work. It can be challenging, but it offers a certain type of fun and freedom. Just think about working with your chosen name, birthing qualities that excite and inspire you, and placing them on the shiny marquee that is your own mind's creation. Why not expect the best?

In order to take action, you will need a clear vision of what you want. That means taking time each day to be quiet and reflect. This sounds more like regeneration than action, but they are two sides of the same coin. In the recent past, I threw my back out. I had just gotten a new exercise bike and I was so anxious to get "back into shape," I didn't listen to my body. I paid no attention to the throbbing in my back.

Instead, I stayed on the bike and kept spinning really hard. The next day, I could barely walk. It was two weeks before I could move without pain. By trying to move into action too soon, I was actually holding myself back.

I once mentored a young woman, Kaylee, whose dream was to be a celebrity hairstylist. When she finished school, she got offered several jobs for what she considered decent money. At the same time, Kaylee's friend who had graduated a little bit before her also wanted to be a celebrity stylist. She urged Kaylee to take a job at one of the salons where the money was "good," and she could start cutting hair right away. Celebrities didn't frequent the salon that had offered her a job, so the haircuts were inexpensive.

Kaylee was excited to have so many job offers. She couldn't wait to put what she had learned into practice when she was offered another job as an apprentice at a famous salon in Beverly Hills. The salary was half of what the other jobs paid, and she wouldn't be cutting hair straight away. She would be sweeping it off the floor instead, perhaps doing a few blow-dries and watching advanced stylists work.

After a lot of reflection and goal-setting, Kaylee decided to take the apprenticeship. Her dream of living without a roommate and getting a place of her own was deferred, but her vocational goals were slowly becoming a reality. This woman did not rush onto the spin bike like I did. She took her time. Today, Kaylee is still an assistant, but she flies all over the world, styling celebrity clients, and she takes over when her boss is traveling to New York or London. The tips she gets are twice what her friend makes in a day. The salon is growing, and it won't be long before she is a stylist in her own right.

I invite you to approach this process with anticipation and a childlike trust that anything is possible, just like Kaylee did. We are so much more than the relentless grind that is modern-day living. We are not defined by relentless lists of responsibilities, the "not enough" and the "way too much." We are more than our sadness and grief. I am more than a mother, wife, writer, yogi, therapist, daughter, sister, teacher, survivor, and friend. My individual health concerns, my addictions and recovery, and my grief and loss do not define me. Nor do the three master's degrees that I earned. I am more than the name I was given, my education, and my family history.

The beautiful and challenging part of The Name Work is that exploring the qualities in the letters of your chosen name gives you the opportunity to discover parts of yourself that you normally don't hold under a microscope. Working with the qualities you unearth is a good way to map out what you want for your life. Don't worry if your name is too long or too short, or if you like another quality with a letter that is not in your name. Don't fret if some of the qualities you find don't seem to apply. Just stay open and willing to work with what you've been given. I believe that no matter how old or accomplished you are, there is room for growth, but first you need to step into action. Despite my great loss, I've had a successful, bountiful life, and I'm still morphing to this day.

Here are some affirmations about Action:

- I take time to pause before moving into action.
- I act according to the Divine Light within.
- I move with ease, grace, and dignity as I meet life's responsibilities.
- My Action is my Divine purpose.
- I am rested and restored as I move into action.
- I feel at peace when I am active.

Questions to ask yourself about Action

- Which activities bring me happiness?
- What are my short-term goals? What do I see happening in two weeks?
- What are my long-term goals? What do I see happening in two months, ten months, or twenty years?
- How do I define success?
- Is Regeneration a part of my action plan? How can I make more time for it?

CHAPTER 12

Creating a Sacred Space

One way to move toward positive action is to tend to your external environment and make sure you're comfortable in your surroundings. Modern and forward-thinking corporations are aware of the influence that the external environment has on internal emotional states. Companies like Google have attempted to create comfortable workspaces. Teachers come in and speak about ways to live in alignment, and places to rest and regenerate are provided. They even offer on-site massages for their employees. The days of stark white stifling cubicles need to come to an end. People are more productive when their environments are expressions of what they love in the world.

Creating a pleasing environment in which to live and work has helped me immensely. Although there is always lots of work to do at my desk, I make certain that my writing environment is filled with the things I love. One way I began to feel better about my clutter was that, instead of beating myself up and telling myself, "You should clean up," I embrace my mess. The late Louise Hay affectionately told her students never to "should" on themselves. That means, "Don't shit on yourself!" It is counterproductive. Her wise words have helped me a lot with my clutter. In time, I learned to look at my stacks of books and affirm, "I have a lot of interests." Today, I see my stuff as an accumulation of love. I must love a lot because things pile up rapidly, but there is beauty in those piles.

I'm not suggesting that things don't fall apart and appear to be out of control, as they did in our yard. It took me many years to go through a closet where I'd put away Kara's things, like welcoming cards, sympathy cards, and her clothes. I avoided this closet for many years. Finally, with organizer Julianna Strickland, we created a special memento box to remember Kara. I also have memento boxes for me and my girls. It's a never-ending process to create a peaceful environment. I used to beat myself up for never alphabetizing my books. Now they sit on my shelves, coordinated in a rainbow of color. It's natural and intuitive to me, and I trust that I'll find what I need to find when I have to.

How is your home environment? Is it comfortable? Is it painted with soothing colors? What's on the walls and the shelves? Do you feel good in your home? How can you make it a sacred space, one that is filled with purpose and heart, reminding you of your ultimate goals?

Creating a peaceful environment that makes you feel good and encourages you to be kind to yourself will make all the difference. Try posting positive affirmations around the house. I recommend keeping hard copies of poems or inspirational messages. Care for a house plant to brighten up your sacred space. Try creating an altar that reminds you of the oft-repeated words of spiritual teacher Ram Dass, "Be Here Now." This means staying in the present moment. When faced with the choice of keeping something or giving it away, Julianna encourages her clients to ask themselves Marie Kondo's popular question, "Does it give me joy?" If the answer is no, it's time to let go.

I do yoga in front of my altar, and it helps me feel better about my life. I have pictures of my husband and daughters and lovely renderings of the Hindu deities Hanuman, Ganesh, Shiva, and anything else that speaks to my higher purpose. I also have a picture of my teacher, Ram

Dass, and his teacher/Guru, Neem Karoli Baba or Maharaj-ji, who remind me to be a loving presence and to look for miracles. These images invite me to have love and gratitude for my teachers and my spiritual community. One of Maharaj-ji's more popular sayings is, "Love everyone, serve everyone, and remember God."

If you can't dedicate a room in your home, I suggest you carry around a sacred object like a crystal, a heart-shaped stone, or anything else you find in nature. When you feel overwhelmed, reach into your pocket, spend some time with your object, and remember that all is well. Ram Dass carried Mala beads with him as a reminder to be here now. Or you can find a place in nature that reminds you of your purpose.

CHAPTER 13

When We Feel Stuck

When I was in the worst pain, I opened a book by Martha Hickman, hoping for a reprieve. It was January 1, and I wanted to begin anew. "Everything brushes against the raw wound of our grief," she wrote, "reminding us of what we have lost, triggering memories—a tilt of the head, a laugh, a way of walking."

I felt my jaw clench. Kara didn't get to do any of those things. I would never see her tilt her head, walk toward me, or laugh at a silly movie. I buried the book in a drawer beside gum wrappers and old diaper cream. There were no books that seemed to help. I had read tons of passages for people who had lost loved ones, but most of them were directed toward those who had a chance to have a full life. At least they had memories, I lamented.

Even my rabbi got it wrong. He put together a grief packet for me, trying to take the pressure off. At the time, I felt I should be memorizing the complicated Aramaic mourning prayer, sacred in Judaism, which you recite daily for the first year after a loved one passes. All I could get was *Yid Gadal, Va Yid kadosh shmay Raba*, and then the very end, with *oseh shalom bim ro mav*. The middle just blurred together. My brain couldn't function, but I thought it was my duty as a nice Jewish girl to memorize it.

"You don't have to do this to yourself," my rabbi said. He wanted me to feel better, to give me something useful. Something less challenging. A strand of hope. One day, after a bath, I took out his booklet, lit a candle, and started reading. I was looking for comfort, and in the packet was a poem which detailed a spouse's memories. The words spoke of the very real torment of a bereaved partner. Maybe that was perfect for a widow or widower. But not for Kara. This poem was about someone who had a chance to live past the age of two months, memories of a person who had a body, breathed, and went to senior prom in a silly dress or a tie. Or maybe she didn't go to prom and instead, she partied in a hotel room all night with the other burnouts like I had. I don't remember the specifics. I forget if the passage was written for a husband, a wife, a man, or a mistress. The point was that this beloved departed person had had a bona fide life. I couldn't bring myself to keep reading. And just like that, the pamphlet went into a pile of well-meant sympathy cards. At the time, I felt stifled. There was nowhere for me to go.

I was in despair, and any forward movement was excruciatingly slow, painful, and humdrum. All I could do was count the weeks and the months because that was all I could hold on to. My therapist assured me that the counting would go away, and it did, but at the time, those numbers and days helped glue me together more than words could. The counting didn't relent until it was time. I couldn't will it to go, and I felt so alone in my grief. Then, it just happened one day. I released the calendar and the need to know how many days had passed in such an exact way.

Then there were the moms who told me that they understood my pain. These were women who'd had miscarriages or, even worse, stillbirths. I allowed them to reach out to me, the women society had told to forget it ever happened and move on. How repressive and wrong was that? Our society turns a blind eye to stillbirths. These mourning women were put through the wringer. They didn't have the luxury of a stack of sympathy cards and well-meant messages. So we reached out and embraced each other, woman to woman. They were once swollen and round, in sync with another heartbeat. They should be able to mourn their losses, and our inhumane society tells them to hush up! My heart ached for them. It really did.

One day, I found myself walking on the beach with a grieving mother who had suffered a stillbirth. "I know exactly how you feel," she said, pointing to her belly. She told me that her recent tummy tuck hadn't taken away the pain of her loss. I looked into her doe eyes and felt a solidarity with her. But still, no matter how horrible her tragedy, she didn't understand my pain. She hadn't held a baby to her breast. She hadn't watched her gain weight and she hadn't seen her first smile. She hadn't felt the heat of her scalp and those fine black baby hairs. No, she hadn't been there.

We sat beneath an orange umbrella, sharing our stories, talking about our journeys. We reached out to embrace each other and I felt the sand tickle my toes, but I still felt alone. Everything in my life was black-and-white back then. I wanted someone to understand my pain entirely. Not just part of it. I had lost an entire child. I wanted to accuse and scream, "You don't get it. You don't understand. You are ill-equipped." But I couldn't go there with that poor mama who never got to hold her living breathing baby. She only got to hold a lifeless infant corpse to her chest.

I felt alone, but I couldn't deny that she was suffering, too. That moment, frozen in time, helped me glimpse our collective suffering. It took me out of myself and my own grief just a little. From my vantage point, human experience is a trek, whether it's the loss of an infant, addiction, aging parents, unruly teens, mental illness, lost possibilities, war, abuse, famine. These days, I understand more completely that there are a myriad of ways we mourn and that to live this life means we can't escape loss.

As the years rolled on, I got less black-and-white about things. I realized that no two people's grief is going to look exactly the same, and some things just don't help. In twelve-step groups, they encourage you to "look at the similarities, not the differences." Today, that is more possible for me to do. Our stories, our fingerprints, the snowflakes that fall on us are all different. There are those who feel relieved after the death of a loved one because that loved one was also an abuser. Or perhaps there is a sense of relief after losing someone who is terminally ill.

The shock of unexpected grief shows up in lost plans and possibilities, of entire chapters ejected, burned, or smashed to bits. Grief and mourning can get convoluted, stunted, or frozen and come out in ways that feel wrong. For example, I have read that some victims of rape experience orgasm during the assault and traumatic memories can elicit the same response. Our bodies and our minds can seemingly betray us.

Right after Kara died, I couldn't feel the enormity of it. My stomach was still swollen, my C-section scar was warm, red, and tender. During that time, I went to see a healing practitioner who played a CD on grieving. I was a zombie. It was all a black screen. I couldn't picture anything. None of it. I couldn't recall Kara learning to suck, her cherubic chin, her eyes, or her face. Images of her swirl through me now as I type. I picture her sleepy eyes, sometimes wet with tears. I see myself watching her first smile. But back then, all I could picture was my first big loss, the passing of my precious dog, Molly. Was I a monster? Why couldn't I remember my baby back then? I understand now that Kara's loss was too much to bear. For my own safety, it became an inaccessible file, an erased tape.

At that point in my fog, all I could summon was the neighbor's dog who everyone knew was mine. I was seven and energetic, and her owners were old and tired. Molly was all ears, and she gravitated to me. I hadn't allowed myself to grieve that sweet basset hound's death at the time, but it showed up for me on a massage table thirty-plus years later. I remembered her long floppy ears. The way she would roll over and let me pet her for hours. The neighbors would have to come over and literally drag her out of our house. She loved me so much, she followed me on my walk to school. "She wouldn't have died if you hadn't let her follow you in the street!" I told myself. I can still hear those words and feel the blame if I let it. It took me thirty years to get in touch with that. There are so many stories just waiting to come out and be expressed if we let them.

Joanne Cacciatore's book *Bearing the Unbearable* is a collection of stories on grief, including her own story, that helps us get in touch with our own. As I sit here making sense of my pain, I commit to constructing a positive narrative, but I have to say that positive doesn't always mean pretty. It comes out crooked and sometimes there are no words that can do it justice. I encourage you to string the words together anyway. To take what you like and leave the rest. Don't throw it all out. Keep the car on the road. Weave together new words and phrases that speak to you. The Name Work will help you with this process. Know that you have a tender heart even if you can't find it. Even if these words do nothing, you are okay. There is no right or wrong way.

CHAPTER 14

The Name Work for Survivors

In order to heal and really engage with The Name Work, we may need to disengage from abusive relationships or toxic family patterns. When we change the way we interact with and react to negative forces in our lives, our personal traumas and tragedies can morph into something new, informed, and inspired.

When I compare my struggles with those of Mother Nature, I think about a worm that gets cut in half. The worm can still grow and begin a completely new life after it has been sliced. The Name Work offers us a chance to become like children who dig in the mud as we unearth what is unpleasant and offer ourselves a remedy.

When we ask ourselves the tougher and more challenging questions that arise from our chosen qualities, we begin to shine a flashlight on our darkness and despair. We can see what's squirming around in our consciousness, label it, and create a healing narrative. Perhaps you've already done the digging and know that you've been victimized. Maybe you can't remember the details, but you have an unsettling and disturbing feeling that follows you around. It doesn't matter if the memories are clear or vague. What matters is whether or not you're letting the abuse, the trauma, that gray feeling of depression, angst, or despair, destroy your life.

It's common in some self-help and wellness communities to say that anger and resentment are like swallowing poison we intend for someone else. Many of us have felt the effects of taking that bad medicine. We've held onto a sense of rightness and lamented that someone has done something that has caused us pain and suffering. The inner dialogue may go something like this: "I'll show them. I'll teach them. I'll prove my case and win the argument. They are sick! They don't care at all. This can't stand!"

Our thoughts race and we stew over them. Some of us plot revenge. But many spiritual teachers have said at one point or another, "Would you rather be happy or would you rather be right?" If we want to be happy, we need to tend kindly to our wounds and our negative thoughts. The Name Work affords us the chance to begin the process of letting others have their own narratives, even when their opinions may in fact be twisted, stilted, crazy, sinister, abusive, or just plain wrong in our eyes.

When we admit that we are angry, hurt, or filled with resentment, we can begin the lifelong and beautiful process of becoming our own best friend. We can begin to let go of the dream of having our grievances heard and being understood. The sting of being called selfish or crazy by others no longer hurts as much when we love ourselves enough to set boundaries and value our life's journey. Through The Name Work, the label "selfish" that we internalized can become "self-care." The affirmation becomes, "I love myself and I set healthy boundaries. It's okay to say no and take care of myself." The label "crazy" can become the beautiful quality, Unique. We can affirm, "I value my unique perceptions and my own life story. It's okay for me to have my own ideas, values, and opinions."

A dear friend of mine, who had a very abusive sibling, says that abuse is like having "love with razor blades." She means that, in order to stay close to the abuser whom we love, we leave ourselves open to the weapons they wield. But once we begin the process of shining a light on our darkness and working with the luminous qualities we discover through The Name Work, those stab wounds transform into little "pin pricks" and it's easier to find our equilibrium.

Here is The Name Work for the word "life."

> **L** is for "life." I honor my life by moving away from abusive relationships.
>
> **I** is for "intimacy." I learn to be my own best friend by becoming intimate with myself.
>
> **F** is "faith." I am willing to face my fears. I have faith in myself.
>
> **E** is for "empathy." I treat myself with tenderness and empathy.

When I was a child, I tried to hide my hurt from the world. Vulnerability was not admirable, and I was ashamed of it. I felt that my hurt and my brokenness said something bad about me. The truth is, I had taken someone else's "jagged little pill" and internalized the messages of being "not good enough." I didn't know at the time that the self-loathing was not mine. It belonged to my abusers. In the world of clinical psychology, this is called projection. I had taken in their negativity.

Have you ever been in the company of an angry or anxious person and suddenly started to feel ill at ease? If you have a good set of boundaries, their anger, sadness, or anxiety can't reach you. If your boundaries need work, you can become ill at ease, angry, or anxious.

One hot day when I was around ten, I wanted to buy an ice cream cone from a store in the center of town. I walked across the street with a pit in my stomach and, like clockwork, there he was as usual, the neighborhood bully, calling out to me while I was cutting across the blacktop kickball courts. I desperately wanted that ice cream, and I wanted to play the Pac-Man machine at the store, but I needed to cut across that court to get where I was going. He stood there like a roadblock, shouting slurs at me. I wanted him to like me, to tell me I was pretty. Instead, he shouted, "Lily, you have scabs on your pussy."

At ten years old, the meaning of what he said didn't register, but I hung my head. Why had he singled me out with so much anger? His face was contorted and red with disgust, and I felt dirty, bad, and wrong. I experienced a kind of self-loathing because I had taken on his toxicity and absorbed what wasn't mine in the first place. Years later, I realized that this young boy was just trying to process the horrid abuse that was happening in his own home. I wonder if his mother had some sort of STD? If she had scabs on her vagina, was she raped? How could a young child refer to my vagina in that way? In any case, whatever left a woman with scabs on her vagina could not be good. But no matter what he meant, he was trying to process way too much for an eleven- or twelve-year-old.

As an adult, I understand that there was a lot of pain in his home. His younger sister would expose her genitalia to the boys in the neighborhood, and the boy took on the role of the male abuser. At the time, none of this made sense. In the wake of these verbal attacks, I felt useless, like old chewing gum stuck to the cement, on my way to the deli.

Being a child was an unsettling and difficult experience for me. As the years wore on, when I heard a group of kids giggling, I was sure they were laughing at me. "Everybody laughs at you, you fool," I thought. That became a running tape in my head, and it took a lot of introspection to heal from it. I felt broken, not enough, and I didn't yet know that I needed to embrace what was hurting me and love myself. Once I did, that became the source of my strength. The poet Rumi said, "The wound is the place where the light enters you." In these pages, I'm showing you how the light entered me through the powerful process of self-discovery that I call The Name Work. When we're willing to find new life after being cut, we can become a wounded healer who can be of great service to the world.

There are many patterns of toxic abuse. I could fill pages with stories of "what they did to me." Most of us can. But I've learned that blame will get me nowhere. It only keeps me trapped in the cycle of abuse. For the purpose of our work here, what is most interesting to me is, how do we identify an abuser? Figuring out where our pain comes from can help us rewrite our own stories and relate to the qualities that we discover in more authentic and helpful ways. If you are a survivor, the following may resonate with you and help you move forward.

Abuse involves extreme levels of narcissism. The question is, how do we spot this toxicity in order to effectively do the work? How do we begin the lifelong process of healing from it? If you confront an abuser with a concern or issue, they will likely turn it around on you and point out something you did.

I had a client with a narcissistic roommate, who left so much garbage in her bedroom that cockroaches began to infest the apartment. She hadn't paid rent since she moved in, and when my client confronted her, the roommate accused her of leaving the front door unlocked six months before. She accused her of making their living environment unsafe. Clearly, this had nothing to do with the cockroach problem or the fact that the rent hadn't been paid.

People in recovery communities call this "blame-shifting." The abuser deflects the confrontation by talking about something completely irrelevant. Abuse is about power and control. Your needs are not of concern to the abuser, and he or she can become enraged, especially if your needs conflict with theirs. If you want something different from what they want, they will fight you. My client eventually had to break her lease, move out, and move back in with her parents. There was simply no reasoning with her roommate.

If you're confronting a family member, it may not be easy. The perpetrator will make you feel guilty in order to get you to serve his or her needs. A family member or close associate knows how to do this well. In recovery groups, they often say, "Family members know how to push your buttons because they installed them."

The abuser's reality is his or her only reality, and it becomes difficult to distance yourself. Just when the victim thinks she is out of harm's way, flowers arrive or the rent gets paid. At the very least, you get showered with flattery. The abuser will always try to come back if there is something to be gained. It could be money, power, prestige, or personal reputation. The narcissistic personality will try to hook you in again and again if there is something to lose when you try to distance yourself. If you manage to move away and you are no longer in their control, they try to suck you back in by any means necessary. This process is called "hoovering" in recovery groups. Once you get sucked back in like a vacuum cleaner, the cycle of abuse starts all over again. It's hard to get off of this bad carnival ride!

"What can I do about this?" you say. If the situation is severe, it may be impossible to begin The Name Work until you remove yourself from the situation entirely. It is important to seek help by calling the police or a local domestic abuse hotline and get protection if you need it. Once you're out of physical danger, you can begin exploring boundaries. You can start by affirming, "I set healthy boundaries for myself. It's okay for me to take care of myself."

When you're dealing with toxic people, it's important to keep your conversations "light and polite." It's a good idea to refuse to talk about other family members and coworkers in their company. Sociopathic or toxic personalities fabricate stories in order to gain control, so it's extremely important to keep things superficial. I had a friend whose father was a prominent professor in a small college town. He told everyone that, when he went to visit his adult daughter in New York, she wouldn't see him. People in his community felt sorry for him and saw him as a "good father." So when the daughter came home to visit, the other family members gave her the cold shoulder. "How could you refuse a visit from your dad?" they asked.

The father routinely bought tickets for himself and his girlfriend to Broadway shows. He left his daughter out. Then, after the plans were made, he'd ask her if she was available during a specific time window. If the daughter couldn't make it, he told people that she refused to see him. Everyone in her town viewed her as cold and unfeeling. The father wrote glowing comments on his daughter's social media posts but criticized her life and her work when no one was there to witness it. There was simply nothing she could do to change the minds of the people around her. Toxic personalities like her father are excellent at recruiting others to their side of the story. In the end, the daughter needed to stop trying to get approval from her community and the other members of her family.

When we engage in grief and recovery programs such as The Name Work, untangling ourselves from abusive patterns is at the core. One such method is "the river rock method," or the "Teflon method." It's about letting it flow, not reacting and letting it stick to you. This means not engaging under any circumstances. When you make your responses neutral, flat, or boring, that disempowers the abuser, who will try to "hoover" or suck you back in. Eventually he or she will tire of it and move on to someone else. It's a good idea to have limited contact or none at all, but this is difficult to do in a toxic family system that might cut the victim off. It can feel very isolating.

Most survivors have been told, either overtly or covertly, that having their our own feelings is not okay. The Name Work teaches us how to celebrate our good feelings and how to move through the difficult ones. When many of us are faced with abuse, we get accused of being too sensitive or misperceiving reality. When this happens, we get out of touch with and unable to trust our instincts. For example, if the abuser is confronted for name-calling, they will deny ever doing it in the first place. Or they might say, "I was just joking. Can't you take a joke?" This kind of manipulation is called "gaslighting." The victim begins to think that maybe he was just joking. But second-guessing ourselves can spill over into every aspect of our lives, so much so that we may not be able to figure out what we really want or need. It becomes difficult to stand on our own two feet, and it can lead to cognitive impairment.

The methods employed in The Name Work can serve as a road map back to the True Self. The Name Work encourages us to ask ourselves the hard questions and take the time to regenerate. The Kara Love Meditation helps us identify our own thoughts so we can begin to change them. These time-tested methods get us back in touch with our heartbeat and breath. Learning to trust our inner thermostat can help us move through the traumatic effects of abuse with love, grace, and dignity. If you feel like someone is gaslighting you, you can use The Name Work to help you learn to trust yourself once again.

This is a popular self-help poem that describes how narcissists think:

> That didn't happen.
> And if it did, it wasn't that bad.
> And if it was, that's not a big deal.

And if it is, that's not my fault.

And if it was, I didn't mean it.

And if I did

You deserved it.

—Author Unknown

If you are familiar with the above, if you try to confront a toxic personality with a grievance and you can't express your feelings, your personal perspective, or a resolution to a problem, chances are you are in an abusive relationship.

How do we distance ourselves from the abuser if he or she is a member of our family or our professional circle? How can you challenge something that feels taboo or carved in stone? Challenging an abuser can feel like you're questioning the literal meaning of the bible in a fundamentalist church. We can feel like we're living under sharia law. Absolute and unflinching. We fear the wrath of the abuser, and we may see them as an evil queen or king who screams, "Off with her head!" We fear our own demise when we challenge what is toxic. If we're dealing with narcissistic patterns, we have to set up boundaries and begin the process of treating ourselves with self-love. We can do this by working with positive self-statements on a daily, hourly, or even minute-by-minute basis. We can't change someone else's reality. We can only change our own patterns of relating. This means allowing someone else to have their feelings about us, even if they're negative or just plain wrong.

When we're trying to distance ourselves within a toxic family, workplace, or relational system, we need to get over our need for approval. Remember that the abuser is masterful at recruiting others to his or her side. When we get away from an abuser, we may lose other family members or an entire extended community. This loss feels like a death and involves a great deal of grief. But we have to put on our oxygen mask first before we can help anyone else. This means fully surrendering and allowing others to hold onto the toxic family narrative, even when it paints an untrue picture of who we are.

I've been on a spiritual quest for over two decades, and I've also run up against spiritual leaders who perpetrate abuse under the guise of being helpful teachers. Those of us who have come in contact with these malignant types have one more layer to heal. Toxic leaders are real. There are lots of Netflix documentaries about the newest cults, and some are more toxic than others. So what do they have in common? They promise you answers to everything. They claim to have the only cure-all method. The leader splatters flattery all over her victims.

As survivors of abuse, many of us have been conditioned to seek love and validation from outside of ourselves, which makes us ripe for more abuse. We fall prey to these people who shower us with affection and promise us that there is a remedy to our pain. We get reeled in with promises of a better life, and we get addicted to the approval and flattery. We are used to being told we are bad, selfish, and wrong, so we gravitate to these leaders who tell us otherwise. Why wouldn't we? But as soon as we get used to the constant loving words, the manipulative leader begins to withhold the validation, and we get stuck in the cycle of trying to earn back their approval. We end up giving the abuser our hard-earned money and time.

In intimate relationships, this is called "traumatic bonding," where the relationship vacillates between approval and rejection or denigration. Are you in an abusive relationship? Do you dread special events, holidays, and occasions that bring the family together? Are you frothing with self-blame? Are you constantly telling yourself that you're not enough? That you're bad or wrong? That no one likes you? Are you being accused of being selfish and not being able to take a joke? Does someone tell you that you're blowing things out of proportion and listening to the wrong therapist? Accuse you of being mentally ill? Of being selfish for setting boundaries? Have you felt like you exist to serve someone else's needs at the expense of your own?

The Name Work can help lighten your load once you are willing to look at the abuse for what it is and give up the idea that you will ever change another person. This work invites you to make the necessary shifts to transform yourself by changing your patterning and giving yourself permission to move away from it.

Twelve-step recovery groups give members "a personal bill of rights," written in a variety of forms to heal from this type of internalized abuse and self-hatred. It can help you find your voice, and it's an important companion to The Name Work as you begin the process of attracting what you want to live your best life.

Here are some important statements in a personal bill of rights:

I have the right to say no and to ask for what I want, to expect honesty and ask for clarification, to walk away when something makes me feel uncomfortable, to change my mind, to take time to pause and regenerate, to turn off my phone, to be safe and treated with respect, to remove myself from an abusive environment, to walk my own path in life, to act in accordance with my own values, to express myself, to believe I am a good person, and to mourn what I didn't get as a child.

Even if you had a good childhood and a well-meaning family and teachers, we all suffer in one way or another. I encourage you to create your own bill of rights by using the one above or making your own. These inherent rights can serve as a True North on your Name Work journey and help you develop a strong sense of self.

Here are a few Name Work affirmations to move us out of victim mode and into survivor mode as we heal ourselves:

- I am enough.
- I take time each day for myself and change my mind if need be.
- I seek out safe environments where I feel protected.
- I practice self-care by walking away from or ignoring what no longer serves me.
- I connect with others on the healing journey.
- I create bonds out of connection and common ground.
- I listen to my body and breath.
- I am on a beautiful journey and am learning to trust my instincts.
- I am kind to myself by taking care of myself.
- I breathe in goodness and I breathe out what no longer serves me.

CHAPTER 15

Body Image

It can be painful to walk around in a body in our youth-obsessed culture. I remember scrutinizing the women in *Glamour* magazine as a kid. Back then, it was all about tight leggings, pink lips, hoop earrings, and rubber bracelets for days, all presented in a sort of neon day-glow mystery.

When I hit my late teens and early twenties, we wore a sea of black tweed, stomping boots, flannels, and vampire lips. High-waist, low-waist, no matter what year it was or who we were, there was a look to be had. We huddled together in dormitories and family rooms, in salons and grocery checkout lines, in airplanes and automobiles, on beaches and bunk beds, in sofas and sleepers, or alone in our rooms at night with a flashlight. Many of us can recall that space where we sat, flipping through magazines, the pages rubbed thin and torn with desires, aspirations, and even angst. I remember inhaling those perfumed pages, hypnotized by the glossy spreads of mostly white women who were thin, young, and beautiful. We were hardly developed physically or mentally as we took in the images that told us what to wear and how to look, the supposed keys to a well-lived life.

When I went to college on the East Coast, I stayed in an old brick coed dorm with a heavy red metal door with a broken lock that separated the boys from the girls. "Your thighs aren't supposed to touch," my friend said, tape measure in hand, as we stood beside each other, staring into a mirror. This ritual of circling the tape around our waists and thighs was routine for us as we kept a record of our bodily circumferences. It was a rite of passage, something we all did together. This winding up of ourselves to look a certain way was very important at the time. I remember beating myself up if my size or weight changed the slightest bit. Never mind the fact that measurements changed with my monthly cycle.

I never fit the fashion trends. I had full hips, thighs, and a large round butt, despite my efforts to look right and be enough. Super thin was in. "I can help you," my friend said. I began to work out daily and starve myself until I got a gap between my thighs. "Don't stop until you want to fuck yourself," she encouraged. "You need to eat a sandwich," another friend said. And after a while I did, as that skinny look was impossible to maintain. Even to this day, with my hard-earned maturity and grounded sense of perspective, my weight still yo-yos, but the pendulum swings a lot more gently now.

Back when I was thirteen, nothing looked right on me. One of my breasts was the size of a small grapefruit and the other was tiny, hanging there like an ugly little sausage, as my grandma put it. It was congenital, she told me, and my mom did what she thought was best. I agreed with her. I wanted to be "pretty," so a plastic surgeon lifted one breast and placed an implant in the other. One month after my fourteenth birthday, I looked in the mirror, happy that I'd been fixed. I felt that I'd been spared having to live with an ugly pair of tits. I didn't know that I was facing an endless cycle of trying to change the look of my body so I would be "good enough." I'd embarked on a lifelong quest for a perfection that I would never achieve.

Many years later, I realize that I was too keen on critiquing the models in the magazine pages. In fact, I was harder on them then I was on myself. I was jealous that I didn't have a thin frame, straight hair, and alluring eyes. Little did I know that many of these girls were younger than I was, barely out of puberty, children without childhoods. They'd been plucked out of cities and small towns by ambitious recruiters who exploited them by putting them in adult situations. These girls were scared and alone, made-up and glossed-over to advertise a standard of beauty that they couldn't even see in themselves.

Today, I'm wiser to the corporate marketing machines. I know about airbrushing and filters. I watch my daughters make TikTok videos with their friends as they praise the slickly spun images of the latest pop stars. How can I protect them? I thank God that today, figures are getting fuller and women are speaking out and saying "Me too." But we still have many rivers to cross.

In 2020, my once-full buttocks are flattened from childbearing, my saddle bags hang, and I am aware that subliminal messages abound. That said, I can still fall prey to them. I think of the famous song by the Red Hot Chili Peppers with lead singer Anthony Kedis belting out the painful truth of feeling like your body is a commodity. He sings:

> *Pay your surgeon very well to break the spell of aging.*
> *Celebrity skin is this your chin or is that war you're waging?*

Courtney Love of Hole sings about the invisibility she feels under that spell.

> *When I wake up in my makeup. It's too early for that dress.*
> *Wilted and faded somewhere in Hollywood.*
> *I'm glad you came here with your pound of flesh.*
> *Oh Cinderella they're all sluts like you.*
> *Beautiful garbage beautiful dresses,*
> *Will you stand up or will you just fall down?*

I've known the unsettling feeling of making myself into an object for someone to adore. I've felt the sting of invisibility as a middle-aged woman. I've felt shlumpy and dumpy with gray hairs peeking through and carrying an extra fifteen to twenty pounds. It's like a slap in the face, a sort of karmic smack, when the doors no longer swing open.

"It's time to let your daughter shine," a friend told me. But what does that mean? It's time to let her sparkle and fall prey to the fashion machine? To the latest craze spun by one of the current pop stars? I thank God for those who have gone before me, writers like Anne Lamott, who so bravely writes about her recovery and shame over the cottage-cheese-like dents in her thighs. She makes it real so I can uncover my own pain, so I can affirm and begin to heal. I'm aware of my addiction to sugar and spice and everything not so nice. I'm more comfortable in my skin now, but not completely.

The difference between today and yesterday is that now I am conscious. I know that the power to change lies within me. I know that a great deal of body image problems come from lack of self-love, so I'm conscious of that, too.

Here's what The Name Work for self-love looks like:

SELF-LOVE

S is for "soul." I honor the unchanging beauty of my soul.

E is for "energy." I have a renewed sense of energy and acceptance when I feed my body with love.

L is for "light." I am filled with lightness of being through the healthy lifestyle that I lead.

F is for "faith." I am strengthened when I face my fears.

L is for "levity." I find ways to smile each day.

O is for "optimism." I fill my mind with thoughts of hope and optimism.

V is for "value." I value the whole me regardless of the number on the scale.

E is for "embrace." I embrace positive change in my life.

In twelve-step meetings, I learned that I am powerless over my trigger foods. Self-love exists independently of how many extra pounds I may or may not have or how "ageless" my face looks. With this knowledge at the front of my mind, I ask myself, "Am I foolish to have botoxed my face to look younger?" My friends call it "self-care," but is it really? Did I make these little changes to feel okay on the outside? To conform to societal standards?

The truth is that I feel better with blonde hair, a botoxed face, and a pair of proportionate boobs the size of two small grapefruits. But I've had to change my implant like a tire over the years. I could have taken it out and let the skin sag, but that plastic breast has been a part of me since I was fourteen. I recently explained this to a friend who was recovering from reconstructive surgery after surviving the horror that is breast cancer. Together we stood in front of the mirror, glad that we decided to keep our roundness.

I had the fat in my belly sucked out at the same time I had my implant replaced. They call it a "mommy makeover." It was a tough decision. A part of me was holding onto my round belly as evidence that Kara had been there, proof that I had been wheeled down to that blindingly bright room to give birth. Today, with the lipo surgery behind me, I feel that the act of removing what I saw as "ugly" to the eyes of the world is sad. A part of me loved my round belly, and I miss the sensations of touching parts of me that are now numb. Was this really what they call a makeover?

I wonder why our society doesn't celebrate the roundness and tenderness that we have, the sagging breasts that once were full of milk. Why is that not a popular image of beauty? Giving birth to Kara was a gorgeous transformation. Why didn't I celebrate the scar, the roundness, and the sagging? Why did I hear the words "ugly and fat" screaming at me when I looked in the mirror? Or "haggard lady." I couldn't make these messages of self-hatred, of not-enough-ness, subside.

Although I had the fat in my tummy sucked out, it didn't suck out the pain. My negative self-talk has moved from my belly to my weight as it tells me I have to lose ten pounds. It's a vicious cycle because happiness that comes on the outside is fleeting. My body renovation doesn't make me feel like I measure up. That is an inside job. I love the serenity prayer that we recite at the end of a twelve-step meeting:

> God,
> Grant me the serenity to accept the things I cannot change,
> The courage to change the things I can,
> And the wisdom to know the difference.

By practicing The Name Work, I'm learning to love myself no matter what the scale says and be gentle with myself, one hot flash at a time. As they say in food recovery groups, "I can make a conscious decision to be sober from foods that trigger me." It's a process and I have yet to achieve long-term sobriety from processed foods and peanut butter as I have from alcohol. But I have a wider and more compassionate perspective which includes a greater amount of self-love. Many of the women whom I most admire are older than me. Many of them are wrinkled and sagging. These babes glow with an inner light.

For me, I'll probably get Botox until the bitter end, but I want to do it with self-love and self-awareness. I'm glad that I do it, but I don't use a euphemism and call it "self-care." I call it "youth preservation obsession." With that in mind, I'm happy, but I look forward to a day when our society values what's happening on the inside as well as the outside.

Clearly, I have miles to go. My hat goes off to women who allow themselves to age naturally. They have pierced through the veil and won't succumb to the false idea that a botoxed face is somehow better. No matter what I choose, I know that, if I pay as much attention to my insides as I do to my outsides, I've begun the process of healing.

Here are some body-positive affirmations.

- I listen to my heartbeat and breath and let my inner light shine.
- I relish the miracle of being alive.
- I nourish my body by eating healthy foods that sustain me.
- I marvel at the miracle that is my body and know that each moment is new.
- I celebrate the beauty of being alive by living a healthy lifestyle.
- I am a beautiful work in progress.
- I am kind to my body and treat it well.
- I look to the inner beauty in others and in the natural world.
- I treat my whole self with kindness in every moment.

PART III

CHAPTER 16

Sitting with Ram Dass

As I grew up and became a young adult, I expanded my thinking and tried out some healing methods that were not readily available in my social and religious community. I know people who find comfort in sticking with one way, but that hasn't been my journey. Have you ever heard the saying by author Susan Jeffries, "Feel the Fear and Do It Anyway"? Much of my healing journey has been about finding the courage to move toward resistance as my heart races and the back of my neck heats up. Embracing fear may seem counterintuitive, but that was where I found a sense of spaciousness and Divine Universal Alignment.

In the coming pages, I'm going to share with you some of my favorite modalities for healing. I hope they will work for you as they did for me. Just remember that teachers are people, too. The "Me Too" movement has brought this to the surface, and there have been a number of shakeups in the yoga and spiritual world. Power can corrupt, so I've learned to trust my intuition when things don't feel right. I urge you to do the same.

For me, wisdom exists in a variety of traditions. This kind of versatility informs my Name Work. I have a daily yoga practice, but the way I approach it has changed over the years. I like to travel away from the familiarity of home, maybe take a day trip to a nearby unfamiliar town to accelerate the healing process. When you do this, when you're out of your comfort zone, you're more apt to see things in a new light.

I'll start with one of my greatest teachers, Ram Dass, formerly Richard Alpert, the famed Harvard professor. He had such a profound influence on my life, I decided to dedicate this entire chapter to him. He affected many people deeply, and he was known as the grandfather of the modern-day self-help and wellness movement. His acclaimed book *Be Here Now* sold millions of copies and inspired a generation to cultivate stillness and be in the moment.

Ram Dass passed away on December 22, 2019. He was in his late eighties, and he had spent two decades in a body that was failing after a massive stroke. How he kept on going is nothing short of grace. Many others would have quit, but he went on, and was surrounded by his friends and caretakers when he died. As I think about it, I still have trouble wrapping my mind around how quickly a life can radically change. Before his stroke, he had plans for a national radio show, and then poof. His plans were gone like a puff of smoke.

When I first went on retreat with Ram Dass in Maui, I had just given up alcohol. And then we lost Kara and I was moving through a lot of grief, groping in the dark, looking for a speck of light. Now that he's gone, I have another kind of tunnel to get through, a different kind of loss. In the weeks after his passing, I couldn't stop watching the news, as I read the heartfelt tributes in the papers and social media. His memory was everywhere, both inside and outside of me.

Ram Dass was a master of the spoken word. His words were his music, but the stroke left him with aphasia, a condition which severely limited his ability to talk and express himself. And yet, even after his stroke, he encouraged me to get out of myself and ask, "How can I help?" In fact, he wrote a book with that title. Even though he was "stroked," as he called it, somehow this limitation didn't matter. He found a way to shine through adversity, to show us "fierce grace." He emanated so much love, I saw the love of my father and grandfather in him. He almost took on their forms in my mind's eye.

I sought Ram Dass out during my Master's in Psychology program in a class that was taught by his former colleague, Sara Winter. When I attended his retreat in Maui, I began a personal and intimate relationship with friends and teachers I would have for many years to come. I met one of my yoga teachers, Mark, and I started a more serious yoga practice. I was so affected by Ram Dass, sometimes it felt like I was hallucinating without drugs in the rustic yoga pavilion where we gathered, an off-the-grid place we called Hale Akua Shangri-La.

As I sat on the floor and looked up at him, I was blown away that a man with "everything" could give away his inheritance. He did that, and it must have blown a lot of people's minds. He started the Seva Foundation, which has restored eyesight to millions of people. After his stroke, he founded the Love, Serve, Remember Foundation, and friends worked tirelessly with him to secure his legacy. They held retreats twice a year, and the archive of his teachings grew. Self-help authors Dr. Wayne Dyer, Michael Beckwith, Sharon Salzberg, Krishna Das, and many other renowned spiritual guides came to Maui twice a year to teach with Ram Dass and make sure he had around-the-clock care. This beautiful man was living proof that the Universe will take care of us if we surrender to its flow. I am in flow when my heart is open to the mystery that is this life.

I heard Ram Dass say that dying, giving up the body, is like taking off an old shoe. But as far as I'm concerned, Kara didn't live long enough for her shoe to come off. She was too new and there were many miles she could have tread in that shoe. I never did get to see her body grow. I had no idea whether her feet would be wide or skinny. Would she be sure-footed or fall off the jungle gym like I had?

Kara deserved a shot at growth. She didn't get it, but it turned out that her passing planted the seeds for mine. Through Ram Dass, I learned that I was more than my emotional states of good and bad, that all of these things were just "grist for the mill" of life. As I meditated with him and practiced kirtan, a sacred chant, I was eventually able to feel something bigger and more spacious than the fear that was engulfing me.

During one of my first retreats in Hawaii, I recall a time when we all sat together in the hills of Maui amidst the fecund greenery. In that sanctuary, I made an unwavering commitment to observe my racing thoughts and not get attached to the story that I uncovered. I had to ask myself, why was I lost? I wasn't sure what I wanted. I was being given the keys to observe it all as a part of this earthly dance. I was encouraged to realize that my negative thoughts had no power over me because I was so much more than this little body and this little incarnation.

When I'm feeling down, I remind myself that Ram Dass continued to teach for twenty years in a failing body after a massive stroke. He found a way to shine amidst adversity. As I type at my desk, I look at a card on my cluttered bulletin board that I got on one of my retreats. The image is of a child in India, deep in prayer. His hands are in the namaste position at his forehead. I see my own childlike yearning in his earnest tears that are streaked across his squinting face.

Ram Dass was a man of great faith, and he urged us to realize that we were all one. He said we were drops in the ocean of God's love. His famous slogan, "Be here now," challenged us to surrender to what was happening in the moment. He encouraged me to ask myself, "Can't I just give up the struggle and be in the moment?"

When I practiced with him and my satsang (spiritual community), I was more able to watch all of it move through my consciousness without making it into "a thing." In fact, I was able to feel the "all" of it, the tremendous joy amidst deep despair without judging any of it. In this space, I felt more connected than I ever had been. And then, like an uproarious fiery crash, it was all over. In this beautiful and cosmic realization, and a newfound community, Kara came and then suddenly went.

Her passing was a horror, and for a long time, I couldn't allow the kirtan chants to touch me. My faith was shattered into pieces smaller than dust. There was simply nothing left. I remember Ram Dass telling the story of feeling so forsaken after his stroke that he took down the images of his beloved Guru, Maharaj-ji, also known as Neem Karoli Baba. This man had been his North Star, his Guru, the reason he wrote his book, and the source of his teaching. But when he had his stroke, he was full of doubt, and he made a decision to dismantle his altars and bury the past.

Ram Dass had been where I had been with Kara's death. And just like me, he would have to say yes to the possibility of Guru/goodness once again. He could not abandon what he had learned, or he would have succumbed to the darkness. And so the pictures of his beloved Neem Karoli Baba, or Maharaj-ji, made their way back up and his altar was reconstructed, both tangibly and in his mind's eye. Because of his willingness to rebuild, he went on to be a light to so many for another twenty years.

Stories like Ram Dass's have given me the strength to rebuild again and again. He's been gone just about two weeks at the time of this writing. I've been overwhelmed and irritable with those I love the most, and I have a nasty case of bronchitis. The grief made its way back into my lungs. Last night, in blessed memory of Ram Dass, I lit the candles on the altar at my friend's house and brought fruit. I knelt down, chanting *Ram Ram Sita Ram* and I placed the fruit below a life-size photo of Maharaj-ji.

One of Ram Dass's more popular quotes is, "We are all just walking each other home." That was what we were doing when we came together to honor Ram Dass's life in my dear friend Badri's Spanish-style casa which had been our temple for the past two decades. He was with Ram Dass before his stroke and in India with the Guru Maharaj-ji before he left his body. Badri has been like a second father to our family over the years. We chanted *Sita Ram, Sita Ram, Sita Ram*, to the beloved husband and wife who depict the masculine and feminine aspects of God. Some call it the soul and body of God. Then we chanted the Hanuman Chalisa, a prayer to Hanuman, whose message is about serving God and humanity. The air was thick as we sat there on cushions and pillows on whatever ground we could find, holding each other in song amidst the sweet aroma of chai and fruit mixed with sandalwood incense. Pictures of Maharaj-ji, Neem Karoli Baba, gazed at us as the candlelight shadows made prayerful dancing images on the walls.

While I was sitting there in the living room amidst the backdrop of moving shadows, I remembered when I lost Kara and lived in fear of God. I recalled the time when I was sunken, a time when chanting offered me no peace. Yet even in that despair, my community was there to pick me up. They stood steadfast in friendship and they held me like no other arms could.

As we all sat together now, in remembrance of Ram Dass, as we continued to chant Sita Ram, our collective humanity merged with the divine in that magical moment. I felt my pain and sadness, but also an abiding love that was bigger than anything I'd ever felt before. It was as if the enormity of my pain, my smallness, my "not-enough-ness," was being absorbed in love. I felt what devotees call "Guru's Grace," and I wondered about the vision I'd had at the gates of heaven on the night Kara died. Was it a part of the cosmic blueprint? That Ganesh's trunk became absorbed into the Wailing Wall? I don't have all the answers, but I am grateful to have found my way onto the path. Thank you, Ram Dass, for your role in igniting this work. May the letters in your name honor the Guru/Goodness and help us all to be of greater service in this world.

The following is how I utilize The Name Work with the letters in Ram Dass:

R is for "reverent." I am filled with reverence for life. I give thanks for the present moment.

A is for "attention." I am centered and responsible by placing my full attention on the task in front of me.

M is for "magic." I embrace the magic of healing and affirm that miracles are possible.

D is "for devoted." I remember to be devoted to feeding people, serving people, and remembering God.

A is for "absolute." My faith is absolute and unwavering.

S is for "soul." I live in alignment with my dharma or soul's purpose.

S is for "surrender." I surrender to the now moment.

As I reflect on the mystical container that was our little memorial, I realize that it has been ten years since I'd felt truly enraptured by kirtan. The ecstatic states it engendered were impossible for me to reach in the depths of my anger and despair over losing my daughter when she was so young. But the veil was lifted and the beauty of this practice reemerged. I am more certain than ever of the truth that Rickie Byars sings, "The way in is the way out."

Unlike Kara's passing, Ram Dass's death offers a freedom I can grasp. Limitless and expansive, I can feel him in my bones and I know that he is free. His body had confined him. His passing has made me even more certain that we are here on a journey to find goodness and meaning and purpose. I recently found an old photo of a much younger version of myself, wide-eyed and glowing, swimming with Ram Dass in a pool in Maui. It was before Kara had died, when a group of other sojourners and I were searching for meaning. I had stopped drinking a short time before and I was desperate to find something other than a bottle to fill my time. I had heard of kirtan, a type of chanting, in which a person could reach ecstatic states without taking a drug. When I started doing it, I found out that it was true. My nightly chanting with the famed kirtan wallahs Krishna Das and Jai Uttal lifted me up. I didn't know that repeating the ancient Sanskrit names for God could take me that high.

As I look at the photo and see myself sitting on the ground, I can envision Ram Dass clearly. His white beard is long, and he is full of presence. I'm in a red tank top with half a dozen sandalwood malas around my neck and one in my hand. I walk around the side of the pool where he's floating and ask him timidly, "Should I study more yoga?"

"Yes, you should study yoga," Ram Dass said, looking at me with his bright blue saucer eyes. Those words helped ignite strong friendships and a sense of community that continues to this day.

In the wake of Ram Dass's passing, I have to acknowledge those who have gone before me, those who have helped me string together these words. Richard Alpert, who morphed into Ram Dass, told us that we were all under his Guru's blanket. He gave us all little bits of the actual blanket during the retreat which were woven into Mala bracelets. Ram Dass laid his life down before his Guru and he did his best to offer us Maharaj-ji's advice to love everyone, serve everyone, and remember God.

I think of him as I write this book. The divine is flowing through me as my fingers peck on the keyboard as on a heavenly verbal piano. As you read this, we are one. Somewhere in the vastness of it all we are connected—Ram Dass and you and me. And we are all together...GROOVY!

It all began there, during those retreats inside rooms in the thick, lush jungle with geckos climbing the walls. I understood the message that we are so much more than the roles we play. I am more than a mother, teacher, survivor, writer, yogi, addict, or sometimes-angry woman. We are all part of a universal dance, or *Lila* as it's called in Sanskrit. I offer you this teaching as I pay homage to the words and examples that resonate with my Highest Soul. May they bring you into greater alignment.

Amen.

CHAPTER 17

Other Healing Modalities

There are many healing modalities available, and some of them are wonderful. But if something doesn't feel right, walk away. Trust your intuition. In Chapter 14, we explored manipulation and malpractice. It's a very real thing. There are leaders who take advantage of their followers. This is happening today in the modern yoga movement, but that doesn't mean they're all bad. Just because there are white supremacist shooters and cult leaders in the world, we can't allow that to stop us from growing and living our lives. There are a large number of healers who do transformative and life-changing work.

In my case, I knew I had to proceed with my healing, and I did it with caution. Below, I've listed some of my favorite modalities for healing. Perhaps they will work for you.

FINDING A YOGA PRACTICE

There are many forms of yoga out there, so look for a practice that is right for your body type, health, and age. With the current trends in our gyms and a number of commercial forms of yoga available, try to remember that twisting yourself into a pretzel without listening to your body or your breath may not be a good idea. That isn't what yoga is meant to be. If something is uncomfortable, please don't do it.

The Kara Love Meditations are my expression of yoga. They come out of the peace I found in moving to this ancient technology which helps me to rest in my own embodiment. I earned my teaching certificate through Mark Whitwell's Heart of Yoga, a practice that transformed my life. Mark was influenced by the work of T. Krishnamacharya, the grandfather of modern yoga, and his son T. K. V. Desikachar. Mark was also influenced by J. Krishnamurti and U. G. Krishnamurti and some lesser-known Tantric masters. I've met many inspiring teachers, friends, and musicians through my friendship with Mark and Heart of Yoga. I've also studied the Bhakti Tradition with Ram Dass, Krishna Das, Jai Uttal, and friends from the retreats and offerings of the Love Serve Remember Foundation. Most recently, I've been studying with Govindas in a lively online satsang. He founded the Urban Ashram, Bhakti Yoga Shala in Santa Monica. He is from the same lineage as Ram Dass.

Our home became an ashram of sorts when I began my practice. We held monthly kirtan sessions where we chanted the Divine Names of God. Piles of shoes and bicycles were parked at our doorstep and the sounds of drums and harmoniums spilled out into the street. Inside, the aroma of chai wafted through the air and samosas from Hurry Curry were enjoyed by all. It was wild and unfettered. This community, born from Ram Dass's love, has helped us through our pain. I thank my yoga teachers for introducing me to my practice.

TRANSCENDENTAL MEDITATION AND AYURVEDA

For my very first retreat, I went to Fairfield, Iowa, to visit a spiritual community established by Maharishi Mahesh Yogi, the guru made famous by the Beatles. I stayed at a place called "The Raj" for a week, where I learned Transcendental Meditation (TM), the art of mantra-based meditation. Each person is given his or her own special mantra, a sacred Sanskrit word or sound that you repeat in your mind to stop the chatter and transcend ordinary consciousness.

When I was introduced to Ayurvedic medicine, a two-thousand-year-old healing science from India, I began to overcome my fear of meditation and being brainwashed. I did what was called Panchakarma, an Ayurvedic treatment that involved the physical application of healing herbs to detoxify my body. I missed my husband David, who was in Kansas City, a three-hour trip away. There were no cell phones back then and I felt disconnected from him, but I stayed. I can see now what a brave move it was for me to drive alone through the cornfields of Iowa, heading toward an unknown place that I hoped might help me.

I was around twenty-five at the time and I had never met or seen pictures of a guru. I wasn't used to relaxing and getting in touch with my inner chatter, so it didn't feel good, and I refused to learn the TM technique at first. My racing thoughts scared me, and I wondered if I was the only one who was jumping ahead, thinking about next week or next year. I feared that my mind would no longer be my own. I was afraid of losing control even though holding on was making me miserable.

Slowly but surely, however, I moved through the fear and pretty soon, I was all in. I got an oil massage every day called Abhyanga that two technicians blended specifically for me, to induce a meditative state. I lay on the table mostly nude, they slathered oil on me that poured out of tubes, and I began to see them as umbilical cords. The two technicians massaged me in rhythm, adept as synchronized swimmers, as I listened to chanting in Sanskrit.

Eventually, I began to enjoy relaxing and listening to a lecture on the benefits of TM. I decided to give it a try even though I feared that I would ascend to some astral plane, never to return. I wrote this in my journal:

Sitting in the quiet sanctuary, I meditate alone for the very first time. I am not sure what's going to happen. I chant my mantra in the quiet of my head and feel a strange connectedness. My breathing gets deeper as my thoughts begin to slow. Bright light enters me and I am not afraid.

As I ready myself to go home, I'm so quiet that I'm shocked by the sound of my own car door shutting. I drive through a tornado. Literally. I watch it swirling in the air. Its purples, pinks, grays, and blacks are new to me. I feel a part of it, of nature. Still, I'm thinking I should be scared of hydroplaning and skidding off the road. My God, I tell myself, it's pouring pitchforks. I should be scared to death. But I'm in Oz, another plane of existence entirely. Cars are pulling off the road to the shoulder, but I am invincible. The calmness feels real, not zombielike. I tell myself, if this is brainwashing, I'm down with the serenity in my head. I am one with the universal storm. I feel otherworldly.

UNITY SCHOOL OF CHRISTIANITY/UNITY VILLAGE AND UNITY TEMPLE ON THE PLAZA

I highly recommend checking out Unity Temple on the Plaza in Kansas City and listening to Reverend Duke Tufty. You can also check out Unity Village in the surrounding suburb, Lee's Summit. Unity has unique teachings but is open to wisdom from a wide variety of writers, speakers, and thinkers who are invited to lecture at their churches and centers. When I listened to bestselling author and spiritual teacher Marianne Williamson speak at Unity Temple on the Plaza, my heart and mind opened. Lee's Summit has overnight facilities and a rose garden where I felt a sense of peace. I was especially impressed with their twenty-four-hour prayer line that I could call when I was in distress. "The Prayer for Protection," written by Unity's own poet laureate, James Dillet Freeman, continues to carry me.

AGAPE INTERNATIONAL CENTER WITH REVEREND MICHAEL BECKWITH

Agape International Spiritual Center, currently located at the Saban Theater in Beverly Hills, has been my home for nearly twenty years. Reverend Michael is an inspiring leader who teaches the power of Visioning. This book would not have come to completion had I not been touched by his teachings, and I'm honored that he has written the foreword. If you are in a bad place, taking yourself to one of his talks can lift you out of despair. Agape has hundreds of licensed teachers who are more than willing to serve. Reverend Michael invites a variety of consciousness-raising speakers to Agape, such as Eckhart Tolle, Marianne Williamson, Don Miguel Ruiz, Neal Donald Walsh, and Judith Orloff. And the music is out of this world.

One of the greatest speakers of our era, Reverend Michael has authored a number of books, and he was a featured teacher in the blockbuster bestseller *The Secret* and the *Heal* documentary on Netflix. He was featured on *Oprah* and on national news countless times, and he sat with the Dalai Lama and other spiritual dignitaries. He founded the Association for Global New Thought and he is co-chair of A Season For Nonviolence with Arun Gandhi. Reverend Michael hosts retreats such as the Revelation Conference in Los Angeles and other gatherings around the globe that change people's lives. He teaches on many online platforms such as Mind Valley and One

Commune and has a weekly radio broadcast among his other offerings. The affirmations for KARA and the qualities you will find in the book came directly through my studies at Agape with the Reverend. It was birthed from the new thought and ancient wisdom garnered from my loving community of "like-minded souls." If you don't live nearby, you can livestream.

RICKIE BYARS

Rickie's music transforms lives and speaks to me as if it were holding me in its arms. She is the former musical director at Agape and founder of KUUMBA, a camp for kids who need a place to heal and grow. Rickie has the voice of an angel as she channels Divine Wisdom. In my weakest moments, all I needed to do was listen to her music and suddenly I felt better. You can see her live in Los Angeles at The Hot & Cool Cafe and at retreats around the world.

INSIGHTLA: FOUNDED BY TRUDY GOODMAN

InsightLA, founded more than twenty years ago, brings together leaders in the field of mindfulness. It offers practice groups called Sangha in the greater Los Angeles area. InsightLA runs a number of charitable programs free of charge. There are specialized practice groups for women, people in recovery, the LGBTQ community, and people of color. InsightLA was established by Trudy Goodman, PhD, vipassana teacher and Founding Teacher. She also teaches residential retreats at centers around the world including Spirit Rock Meditation Center, Insight Meditation Society, and Big Bear Retreat Center.

SHARON SALZBERG AND INSIGHT MEDITATION SOCIETY

Sharon is one of the OGs (Original Goddesses) of the modern meditation and wellness movement. She has studied with many masters and is a leader in the field of mindfulness and lovingkindness meditation. Her teachings are calming and accessible. The author of many books, she is the founder of the Insight Meditation Society and Spirit Rock, along with Jack Kornfield and Joseph Goldstein. In her first book, *Faith*, she talks about her personal losses as a child. I am forever grateful for her willingness to bear witness to my loss. She offers retreats both remotely and in person. Her latest book *Real Change* offers help and healing for these times of collective grief.

BHAKTI YOGA SHALA

Bhakti Yoga Shala was the first yoga studio in Los Angeles to offer weekly kirtan to the public. It is run by Govind Das and his lovely wife Radha, who play kirtan music and practice soul-centered yoga. They are part of the Ram Dass Bhakti Satsang and honor the legacy of Ram Dass through their steadfast devotion to Maharaj-ji and Hanuman. My favorite kirtan musicians have graced this urban oasis, such as Govind Das, Wah, Radha, Jai Uttal, Joey Lugassy, C. C. White, Spring Groove, Josh Brill, Shiva Baum and friends, the Kirtan Rabbi, and David Stringer.

MICHELINE BERRY AND JOEY LUGASSY, DAVID STRINGER AND DEARBHLA KELLY

If you have a lust for spiritual travel, consider a trip with either one of these dynamic duos. Joey Lugassy personally carried a harmonium through the corridors to chant kirtan while I lay in the hospital at Cedars-Sinai. He plays music for our Kara Love Project fundraiser each year. I've traveled with Micheline and Joey to New Mexico, Brazil, the Galapagos Islands, Italy, and Cuba, where they make music and offer cultural immersion through a variety of spiritual practices.

David Stringer is a well-known scholar and kirtan musician, and his wife Dearbhla is also a teacher and yoga scholar. I've attended their local workshops, and I went on a magical trip with them to Dearbhla's birth home in Ireland. David partnered with local musicians there and we were uplifted by blissful melodies and sound.

MARIANNE WILLIAMSON

Marianne Williamson has written thirteen books, four of which were *New York Times* bestsellers. Her teachings on *A Course in Miracles* have uplifted many people's lives, including my own. Her book *A Return to Love* was a game-changer, and I wouldn't be on this journey without her wisdom. My favorite quote from *Return to Love* is:

"Our deepest fear is not that we are inadequate. Our deepest fear is that we are powerful beyond measure. It is our light, not our darkness, that most frightens us. We ask ourselves, Who am I to be brilliant, gorgeous, talented, fabulous? Actually, who are you not to be? You are a child of God. Your playing small does not serve the world. There is nothing enlightened about shrinking so that other people won't feel insecure around you."

Marianne is a political activist who ran for president and participated in several Democratic national debates. She continues to stand for justice. She is founder of Project Angel Food, a volunteer food delivery program that serves homebound people in the Los Angeles area. She also founded the Williamson Institute, which advocates "taking a stand for the life you want to lead." She is known as one of Oprah Winfrey's spiritual advisors.

JUDITH ORLOFF

Renowned psychiatrist Dr. Judith Orloff is a personal mentor and friend. She has given me the courage to bring this book to completion and teaches about the power of empathy and intuition. I had the good fortune to travel with her to visit Ram Dass when she was a part of his podcast. I have personally experienced the power of her teachings both on Maui and at Esalen Institute.

A *New York Times* bestselling author, she conducts workshops, retreats, and private sessions. She is a powerful public speaker. Her newest books, the *New York Times* bestseller *The Empath's Survival Guide* and *Thriving as an Empath,* offer practical tools and strategies for sensitive people. She is a psychiatrist, an empath, and an intuitive healer. She is on the UCLA clinical faculty.

LORIN ROCHE AND CAMILLE MAURINE

Lorin Roche and his wife Camille Maurine are mentors and friends who encouraged the birth of this book right from the start. Together, they authored the groundbreaking work *Meditation Secrets for Women*, a book that was required reading during my graduate studies as I discovered myriad ways to meditate. Roche is the author of *The*

Radiance Sutras, an epic translation of the Vijnana Bhairava, which is a work of soul poetry. The couple hold workshops and retreats around the globe.

LA YOGA

LA YOGA is a friend of the Los Angeles community and beyond. It connects thousands of yoga students, teachers, studio owners, and balance-seekers with information on how to integrate yoga in the modern world. It profiles teachers, features events, showcases people changing communities—like our Kara Love Project—shares Ayurvedic and health knowledge, and goes backstage with musicians, filmmakers, and other artists. Its editor-in-chief, Felicia Tomasko, earned degrees in environmental biology and anthropology and nursing, and certifications in yoga, yoga therapy, and Ayurveda. She leads yoga and Ayurveda classes and champions causes to make the world a better place.

BHAKTIFEST, LOVE SERVE REMEMBER, AND HANUMAN MAUI

At Bhaktifest, the one and only Shiva Baum has been the emcee since the start of this "Spiritual Woodstock" featuring numerous Kirtan Musicians, Spiritual Jam Bands, Teachers and Healers. Held in Joshua Tree, CA, thousands gather in friendship to bring more Bhakti or love into the world. Zoe Kors, Josh Brill, Trevor Hall, M.C. Yogi, Govindas, Radha, Jai Uttal, Adam Bauer, Daniel Stewart, Nina Rao, Bhagavan Das, and Dave Stringer are just a small sampling of some of the folks who play a part in this amazing retreat. Ram Dass always live-streamed at Bhaktifest from Maui when he was in his body. The Love

Serve Remember Foundation and Hanuman Maui are also included here as they offer more intimate offerings. Both of these organizations continue the legacy of Ram Dass.

DENISE KAUFMAN AND ACE OF CUPS

Denise was present at the birth of Yin Yoga and is a leader in the practice today. She is a change-maker and champion of numerous social causes and was part of the first all-female rock 'n roll band, Ace of Cups. Denise is a personal friend, mentor, and guide and if you can catch a Yin Yoga class with Denise you are in luck.

JULIE LEAR

Julie is a registered yoga teacher, Reiki practitioner, and longtime marketing pro who has played an instrumental role in bringing The Name Work to fruition. My best friend of over thirty years, she is our organization's Lead Teacher and a great friend of our Kara Love Project. She has an at-once wise, practical, loving, and holistic vision and a knack for detail like none other! When she's not consulting organizations, she teaches yoga online and at Elephant Tree Yoga in Ipswich, MA.

SHELLEY KARPATY

Shelly is a certified enneagram coach and career guide who I've enjoyed a friendship with for over thirty years. Her personal essays and other writing can be found on Medium, Common Ground, Elephant Journal and LA Yoga.

NATIVE AMERICAN SWEAT LODGE

I was introduced to the sweat lodge at a retreat led by Micheline Berry, spiritual teacher and yoga instructor. Sweating is a Native American practice used for healing and prayer. You sit in a makeshift tent or teepee constructed of tree branches with blankets covering the top as the leader pours water over hot coals to create steam. As we begin to sweat in the pitch-black atmosphere, we pray, chant, and honor our ancestors. The sweat lodge helped me get over my fear of cramped spaces, since we were squished in like sardines. I tried not to panic. "Feeling the fear and doing it anyway" proved to be exhilarating. I felt cleansed when I emerged into the cool night air and gazed up at the stars.

ROPES COURSE AND ROCK WALL CLIMBING

Doing a ropes course and climbing a rock wall are good ways to move through fear. I was on a women's retreat, staying in a yurt, a rounded teepee, when I completed my first ropes course. I remember waking up in the middle of the night to a symphony of insect noises and bird calls that I thought was a tape! I smiled when I realized how far away I'd gotten from Mother Nature, and I was so glad to feel her again.

In order to learn to trust the group, I put on a blindfold as they led me in the right direction. I was asked to do things like falling backward, trusting that the other participants would catch me. I climbed tall trees with people holding me in case I fell. It was heartening to see that women who I thought were fearless were afraid of some parts of the course. I recall a woman fifteen years my senior who had a wavy head of long graying blonde hair and wore flannel shirts. A warrior who knew no bounds, she was in front of me as we climbed the tall oak tree. Seeing her shaking, wondering if she could make it, gave me strength.

"You can do it, Rochelle!" we all called out to her.

She made the trek, and when she finally ziplined down, we encircled her and gave her a group hug. She helped me understand that we all have sweet, gushy, vulnerable parts. We all need to be rocked to sleep sometimes and fall into someone's arms.

WALK A LABYRINTH

A labyrinth differs from a maze because there is only one way in and one way out. Before you enter the labyrinth, you say a prayer and set an intention. The goal is to walk the circular winding path to get to the center, which symbolizes heaven and provides a metaphor for a spiritual quest. You leave something in the center, like a seashell, a crystal, or a flower, and you walk back out again, following the same path. One of the oldest labyrinths, in the Chartres Cathedral in France, is reputed to have been in existence as early as the year 1200.

When I entered my first labyrinth in the wild grasses of Blue Springs, Missouri, I wondered how long it would take to walk this seemingly endless path. But once I gave up the mental struggle and stopped asking myself when it would end, I slowed my gait, surrendered to the moment, and took in the beauty around me.

Since then, I've walked labyrinths at an Episcopal church in Jackson Hole, in Black Rock City at Burning Man, at Miraval in Tucson, Arizona, at the exclusive Golden Door Spa outside San Diego, and at Canyon Ranch in Tucson.

ESALEN INSTITUTE

Esalen Institute in Big Sur, California, has long been at the heart of the human potential movement. Psychologist Fritz Perls worked out many of his theories there. Donovan sang. Allen Ginsberg read his poetry. Today, Esalen has continuing education workshops in a variety of disciplines. There is an art barn, a natural hot spring where you can rest and rejuvenate, sustainable vegetable gardens, massages, and a breathtaking view of the Pacific Ocean.

David and I went there several weeks after Kara died. I sat in the hot spring baths, my C-section scar still raw and tender, gazing up at the stars. One of the biggest meteor showers I've ever seen took place that night and people were cheering as if we were watching a fireworks display. I was too full of shock, pain, and numbness to feel anything. I don't think I'd fully admitted to myself that Kara was gone, and I was in a living nightmare. But now, in hindsight, perhaps my precious girl was winking at me from the heavens.

KRIPALU CENTER

Kripalu offers a variety of workshops in yoga and the healing sciences. I attended a workshop there with Jai Uttal during winter, when snow decorated the sprawling lawn and trees. It is quiet, peaceful, and worth exploring.

TWELVE-STEP PROGRAMS

Twelve-step recovery programs have helped me on my journey. I wouldn't be the person I am today without them. There are twelve-step programs for just about everything. You don't have to be an alcoholic or addict to benefit from these wonderful programs. I give thanks to my sober sisters on the path. You know who you are.

TAKE AN ONLINE CLASS

Many of the teachers that I have mentioned here and throughout the book offer online classes. Some of them are even free of charge! You can also find their talks, classes, and music through a simple google search.

WALDORF SCHOOLS AND ANTHROPOSOPHY

When I didn't know where to turn as a mother, I was blessed to find the Westside Waldorf School's early childhood program. Founded by Rudolf Steiner, the Waldorf curriculum emphasizes the whole child and helps them recognize their connection to the natural world. It provides opportunities to pause, regenerate, and celebrate innate alignment.

INTERNATIONAL SOCIETY FOR KRISHNA CONSCIOUSNESS (ISKON), LOS ANGELES

When I was working a stressful job, I enjoyed the vegetarian food at this wonderful Krishna Temple during my lunch hour. I found calmness there and listened to devotional chants. I still find peace when I chant the mantra, *Hare Krishna, Hare Krishna, Krishna Krishna Hare Hare. Hare Rama Hare Rama, Rama Rama, Hare Hare.*

I admire how they feed hundreds of people at the lively and magnetic Festival of Chariots in Venice Beach each August. I had the great opportunity to meet one of the movement's gurus, Radanath Swami, at my friend Narayan's home, which also serves as a temple. He is the inspiration behind ISKON's free midday meal, which feeds 1.2 million school kids across India.

THE KIRTAN RABBI

Rabbi Andrew Hahn, PhD, introduces Jewish wisdom to people of all backgrounds. He is a soulful man who brings depth and meaning to the Hebrew prayers that I learned as a child, and to my practice of Judaism today.

CHAPTER 18

Our Precious Gifts

Moving into action for me meant having our babies. We had tried several rounds of in-vitro fertilization before I had Kara and another cycle after she died. Each session felt like a boxing round because my personality was completely overwhelmed by chemicals. Injections of hormones were tough enough for a healthy person, but I after I lost Kara, I was in the depths of grief. I may not have had a fat lip and bloodied face, but I was beaten up emotionally. The cocktail of compounds was sending me into oblivion. It was like having a computer virus. I wasn't operating normally, and when my period came back each month, I remembered how it felt to be me.

When I got into my own flow and felt normal again, I was still aching with grief. I was grateful that I was no longer under the influence of synthetic hormones, but I was miserable being without a child. I felt robbed. I'd imagined that I would give birth by age thirty-five or thirty-six and have a huge fortieth birthday celebration. It all fell apart. My friends threw me a fortieth luncheon, but it felt wrong, partly because I'd had in-vitro that morning and I was a mess. I felt like an emotional basket case during that luncheon. I wished I'd cancelled it as I drove there. I couldn't even appreciate the flowers on my table. My friends were loving and supportive, but all I could think about was my little girl who had died. Everything was off-kilter. It was like living in hell.

After my fortieth birthday, I continued going to my home group twelve-step meeting each week, but I was a wreck. I couldn't sit still. I moved around the room like a lap dog, begging for affection. I felt like I was talking nonsensically, and I didn't have a grip on what was happening around me. When I wasn't in a meeting, people asked me when I was expecting, since my stomach was still raw and swollen.

During one meeting, I was sifting through the coffee mugs, looking for my favorite, the rainbow one. It was already taken, so I settled on a plain cup with most of the decal worn off. That made sense. I didn't feel colorful, and the sound of children playing outside reminded me of my loss. As I started to make my way from the kitchen to the meeting room, a friend greeted me. She had had similar fertility struggles, but now she was holding a baby.

"I didn't know you got pregnant," I said.

She looked at me and smiled. "I didn't. I adopted. You know, you should really think about it. I tried in-vitro eight times and that shit makes you crazy."

"Tell me about it," I said. I gazed at her adorable infant, who was not even a year old. "Thanks," I said. "I'm going to look into it."

I once heard someone say that adoption described a family that was bound together not by blood, but by love. I liked these sentiments, so I did The Name Work for the word "adoption" to see how it felt.

> **A** is for "Allow." I allow goodness to flow into my life.
>
> **D** is for "Divine." My family is divinely appointed.
>
> **O** is for "Optimism." I look with optimism toward the future while embracing the now moments.
>
> **P** is for "Parenthood." I honor my chosen expression of motherhood and I parent from a conscious and loving place.
>
> **T** is for "Truth." I honor my family's individual and collective truths.

I is for "Intimate." I create an intimate loving home.

O is for "Open." I am open and I listen to my children's needs.

N is for "North Star." The love of family is my North Star.

As I stood in my sunroom, I knew that I wanted to pursue adoption. I talked with David, he agreed, and a few days later, we began the process. We filled out mountains of paperwork and things moved quickly. In November, we got a call from a woman in the Midwest who could not keep her unborn child. A few months later, we were there when our daughter Marcelle was born. I cut the umbilical cord with a shaky hand and I held a chubby, red, wrinkled infant in my arms. She was ours. I have infinite gratitude for the beautiful birth mother who took a chance on us. I was still in terrible grief, but she trusted me and David to parent. Her decision to choose us helped to lead me out of the darkness.

When we got Marcelle home, it wasn't easy. I was still overwhelmed by clouds of numbness and despair. I was afraid of my new life, afraid of the unknown, afraid of more tragedy. Twice the size of our Kara, Marcelle was a unique being and could never replace the child I lost. *Nor should she*, I told myself. Although her birth filled me with a sense of hope, I felt unspeakable terror at night that gave way to a soul-sucking numbness. I slept through the night soundly, near-comatose, telling myself that if Marcelle lost her life and breath like Kara had, there was nothing I could do to save her. In those first few months, I left the night shift to David and our nanny, Norma, who was there to pick up the pieces.

David was overjoyed to take over, attending to our new child's every need. He had been working a lot after Kara was born and he felt he had missed out on much of her short life. He had retired from his sales position when she died and now he was committed to spending quality time with our new baby.

When she was two months old, I took her to a mother-and-child group looking for support, terrified to be alone with my child. I'll never forget the long halls in that building and sitting in a circle on plush carpeting with a few other first-time moms. We were all wide-eyed and uncertain for one reason or another as we went around the circle and introduced ourselves.

Marcelle started crying almost immediately. I reached into my diaper bag and pulled out a bottle. She rejected it, so I tried to rock her. This went on for several minutes, and I became panicked when I was unable to soothe her. One of the rules of the group was to stay in the circle so the "expert" could help us move through whatever challenges arose. Everything in me wanted to leave the room, but I stayed, obeying the rules. I thought I saw the group leader give me a nasty look, but I told myself that I was just nervous.

Marcelle's crying went on for what seemed like an eternity. I was close to tears myself when the so-called expert asked us to leave the room since my baby was what she called "too disorganized." I never went back to that group. I doubted my capacity to be a mother and the experience left me feeling worse than before.

It was another four months before I sought outside help again. I continued to fear being alone with Marcelle, consumed by thoughts of death and loss. I brought her to another mother-and-child group, run by the local Waldorf School, and it was different. It wasn't stern or cold, and I didn't feel judged. There were meditative moments, and we even sang to the fairies.

I remember that first day, sitting in a beautiful room with wooden furniture, hand-made dolls, and silk tapestries that hung on beautiful pastel-painted walls. The leader sang an opening song:

"Gentle Fairy, come join us, come join us today, and dance in a garden where we work and play." It was beautiful and magical.

I remember pouring my heart out to the group leader, Miss Monique, telling her my story and talking about my fears. I sat on a hand-woven cushion and sobbed, "I'm a terrible mother." The tears wouldn't stop as Marcelle crawled on the floor, making her way to the play kitchen. One of the women said, "You're doing the best you can. You've been through so much. Please stop judging yourself. You're here, right where you need to be."

She was right. I found a sense of wonder at being a mommy with a baby. Marcelle was in my lap as we sang nursery rhymes and I rocked her:

Rock, rock, rock your boat, gently side to side.
If you see a crocodile, don't forget to hide.

Marcelle and I both giggled and she begged for more.

Now, more than eight years later, our relationship is strong and Marcelle is a sweet spirit who doesn't need to talk to fill up silent spaces. She's comfortable in her own skin. We bake together, and watching her dance is a joy.

Soon after Marcelle came to us, we adopted another baby, Sally. She had a tough birth and she was ill for a few weeks. Like Kara, she spent her first week in the NICU at Cedars-Sinai Hospital where they monitored her closely. Luckily, her situation was not the horror story the doctors were initially concerned about.

This time I faced my fears. Perhaps it was because Sally was so sick, I couldn't turn away. Maybe it was the fact that I didn't want to miss my chance at bonding with her from the start. Or it might have been the renewed sense of confidence I found at the Waldorf School. Whatever it was, Sally's illness subsided and our bond was there from the start.

My girls are very different. Marcelle is gentle, quiet, and reserved in the most wonderful way. She's had a strong focus since she was two years old. Now she is an aspiring dancer. She enjoys watching "how to" videos in her spare time and she loves trying out new recipes that require patience and detail.

Sally is the opposite. She's wild and unbridled, friendly with everyone, and she has a sense of sweeping adventure and magic. She enjoys dancing with her sister, but playing with dolls, drawing, and dress-up is where she expresses her creativity. She changes her outfits five times a day and her collection of princess costumes is astounding. I sometimes worry about spoiling her. She smiles a lot, and she gives herself and her dolls haircuts. Her creativity sometimes gets her into trouble, but I'm happy to be on the adventure with her.

I also enjoy a family friendship with a twelve-year-old boy whose mother died when he was young. David and I are close to his father, and now we have an extended family.

I hope my children will always remember their connection to the Divine Mother/God and the Universe so they have a gentle initiation into adulthood. I hope this life is kind to them and, when it knocks them down, that they will retain a sense of hope that all is well. I am beyond grateful to my friend who encouraged me and David to take the journey and adopt. Today our families play together, and we are connected and have full lives.

Epilogue

Losing Kara left me with a kind of grief that was as profound as the ocean. I know that I will never experience it fully. When I feel the sadness, I go within and witness what moves me. I have learned that I can't bypass grief, but I have to stay with it. No matter how much I explore this reality, there is so much more to know. It seems like I've only scratched the surface.

I hope you'll find peace, and I invite you to take what you can from my healing process. As you explore the qualities found in your name or the name of a loved one, I hold the vision that they will serve as your North Star. If you need inspiration, there is an index of qualities at the back of this book and some pertinent questions to awaken the part of you that wants to evolve and birth your life's purpose.

Since I began the Kara Love Project and created The Name Work, we have been able to help hundreds of people. Kara's name has taken on new life and has enriched my own as I act as a guide for people who choose to live consciously. We've raised thousands of dollars to help underserved people at home or abroad who are facing life challenges and are marginalized locally and globally.

We are committed to creating quality community programming that supports the work we do. We conduct coaching sessions and trainings and we hold workshops. My husband and I have made a conscious decision to stay in our home and to embrace the complexity of living again. Here on this land, we have found joy in the same place where we once felt unspeakable sorrow. As I take in my surroundings today, I feel a smoothness, a softness. Colorful prayer flags hang between two trees in our yard that remind me of the beautiful fundraisers and events that we have on our lawn. I can see us all swirling to drumbeats and dancing in the moonlight. I look again and the flags are motionless, and then they move with the next gentle breeze. A lot of good happens here.

When I think of the orphaned girls in Nepal who gave us the flags, I remember walking the dusty colorful streets of Bhaktapur. I breathe a sigh of gratitude because I am fulfilled by the connection we made with the Unatti Foundation. Girls who are taken in by the Unatti Home for Girls have a warm bed and regular meals, they get an education, and they have a chance for a better life.

As I write these pages, the colorful cloth sways softly, almost knowingly, in front of two huge sprawling pines that were most likely here before I was born. Have they borne witness to my struggles and triumphs in some mystical way? A neon soccer goal sits under the trees and flags, reminding me that this yard is a haven for the living, a place where people come to heal and to feel their interconnectedness with other human beings. This is the place where we have had birthday parties, camps, fundraisers, holiday get-togethers, and even a wedding.

I would not have come as far as I have without the loving support of my husband, David. He has stuck by me through it all. We met when we were both nineteen and we've found our way together, lugging sofas up four-story walkups in our earlier days. When I decided to stop drinking, he supported me and has taken the full ride with me. He is a loving father who isn't afraid of being a nurturer. In fact, he has taught me most of what I know about being loving and compassionate. It hasn't always been easy, but we've remained true to each other in spite of our mistakes. David was and always will be the dearest friend I've ever known.

We're repainting our living room today. Everything needs to come off of the shelves and walls in order to create something new. On the top shelf is a montage of pictures in a frame, images of Kara, our sweet baby girl. In one of the photos, she is looking up at me with her round cherubic face, wide-eyed with wonder, in a pink onesie. It was a precious moment. My girl had gained a full five pounds before she died, and she was supposed to be healthy. I still ask, *Why did she go?* My sadness is boundless, like deep space.

I heard a scientist hypothesize that we carry ancestral memories in our DNA. Perhaps my grief for Kara taps into memories from past lifetimes. Has my sadness put me in touch with other areas in my life where I could be more fulfilled? Is it the collective societal sadness that I feel? It's helpful for me to ask myself these things, as they connect me to a shared human experience. We live in a society that frowns upon these kinds of questions. We value youth and agility and freezing the lines out of our faces. We do our best to walk with a spring in our step when our knee throbs or we ache inside. We don't talk about our pain, our grief, our misery. Instead, we put on a façade that everything is alright.

I would like to challenge us all, myself included, to relinquish our collective need to pretend. Life is scary at times, and we need to love and care for ourselves and each other. As Ram Dass says, "We are all just walking each other home."

May the Divine Wisdom found in all of our names make our lives and our world just a little bit better. May this work connect us all in love as we move and groove and have a life. May your chosen name offer you a sense of renewal and peace, now and every day. Om, Shanti, Shalom.

Pandemics and Other Collective Tragedies

It's May 2020, a few weeks shy of what would have been Kara's eleventh birthday. My joints are creakier, but my life is fuller, in spite of it all. For the most part, I've surrendered, and I work with what I've been given with a grateful heart. Still, there are days when our fragility as human beings smacks me in the face and fills my heart with fear. Sometimes my body feels like a helpless bag of blood and bones.

We are moving through a tragedy of global proportions. Covid-19 has appeared on the scene, hundreds of thousands are dead, and the loss of life is staggering. Millions of us are in lockdown, not knowing what's coming next. In Guatemala, families in quarantine who have no food are hanging white flags at their doors, a signal of hope that some morsels will arrive. Syrian refugees and the homeless here in our own backyard are huddled in the streets, wide open to the sinister elements. In Italy, they don't know what to do with the bodies.

Against this backdrop, having a safe home seems like a slice of heaven, even though our children have been yanked out of school and milestones like graduations are happening remotely on a computer screen. Our daughter will not be able to compete in the dance competition that she worked tirelessly for months to prepare for; her feet are blistered for a reward that won't come. Ceremonies of all kinds have been cancelled. Concerts and caravans are done. Life as we knew it is over for now. Or is it just plain over? Nobody knows. The tunnel in which we collectively find ourselves is dark and uncertain. The gap between rich and poor is wider than ever before and people of color are especially vulnerable to violent systemic abuse. For me, The Name Work is serving as a blueprint to move through it all with more peace and dignity.

When I look back on my own life experience and the development of The Name Work, I think of my twelve-step recovery. Step One in my twelve-step program is that we admitted we were powerless over alcohol and that our lives had become unmanageable. Today, our way of life feels unmanageable, and I have to admit how powerless I am over this pandemic and over all acts of Mother Nature. The internet is my lifeline and when it crashes, it's hard for me to stop my mood from crashing, too.

There is an overwhelming sense of powerlessness when it comes to fixing the pain. I just need to surrender. I'm not Jesus, and I can't make this go away. But, similar to the aftermath of Kara's death, I can choose to grow rather than shrink from the societal troubles we're facing. This means taking my Name Work Practice seriously, especially at this time, and limiting contact with toxic people. Many of us are meeting remotely and I thank God for my spiritual communities and the miracle of the internet. We gather together on the computer screen like a bunch of Hollywood Squares, with messages of hope.

Here are some of my thoughts as I delve deeply into my individual and collective practice. The Name Work that happens around the pandemic looks something like this:

> **P** is for powerlessness:
> I accept that I am powerless over this pandemic and I do what I can to stay safe, healthy, and maintain a positive state of mind.

A is for acting as if:

  When darkness sets in, I act as if everything will be alright. I am a light for myself and others.

N is for noble:

  I look to what is good and right in this world. My path is noble, courageous, and true.

D is for direction:

  I surrender to not knowing and find inner direction through becoming still. Out of this stillness I am more readily able to align with positive changemakers and work towards creating a just society.

E is for ember:

  I stoke my inner fire with the divine embers of positive thought, deed, and action.

M is for miracle:

  I look for the little miracles in daily life.

I is for intelligence:

  I trust in my innate intelligence and perceptions. I trust myself when something doesn't feel right.

C is for center:

  I take time each day to go within and find my still center, whether I am on the front lines or distancing at home.

I'm so sad for people who have lost everything. A hairdresser friend and her child are on food stamps. Others are worrying about keeping a roof over their heads. I have immense gratitude and fear for people on the front lines. I have a friend, an ER doctor with a wife and daughter, and another, a doctor as well, who works with the homeless. Doctors in our family are in the midst of it, and I worry about our aging parents. How are they coping with the stress? When I think of people who are in the line of fire, the inconvenience of wiping our bums with paper towels is diminished.

I went to a Zoom memorial yesterday. I can't stop thinking about my friend who couldn't have a traditional memorial for her child. Her family and friends couldn't wrap their arms around her. I ache for her family, the loss of her child, and all of the people who are dying isolated and alone. In all of this, I remember my therapist Marilyn's advice to keep the car on the road.

Our previously gridlocked freeways are empty at rush hour as we take a trip to our family home in the desert to have a swim and pick up some vital supplies. It feels post-apocalyptic, but we have toilet paper now and my kids are alright. They splash in the pool while we try to forget for a moment. They giggle as they duck down in the water, but the following words make me shudder.

"Ring around the rosy, pocket full of posy,
Ashes, ashes, we all fall down."

That little song that was written during the bubonic plague in 1342 has never felt so real. Back then, people wore herbs around their necks and in their pockets to stave off death. Today, my pockets may not be full of posy, but I am taking healing herbs and hand sanitizer is always nearby. Whatever is happening, we have to go on, grateful for our blessings and keeping in mind that some of us are facing dire suffering. We must work together to become better, stronger, wiser people. There really is no alternative. I hold the vision that we will eventually rise above it all. May the practices that make up The Name Work guide you, no matter what you're facing.

From A to Z

A

QUALITIES

Agreement, Ambition, Alignment, Attentiveness, Affection, Action

SAMPLE AFFIRMATIONS

- **Agreement:** I live in *Agreement* with my life by having the courage to take a stand and disagree. By disagreeing, I come into alignment with what agrees with me.

- **Ambition:** It is safe for me to be *ambitious*. Going for my good helps me to grow and be a beacon of light to those around me.

- **Alignment:** No matter how dark it may seem, I affirm that there is light at the end of the tunnel of darkness. I affirm that God is good and the Universe is in perfect *alignment*.

- **Attention:** I am centered and responsible by wholly placing my *attention* on whatever task is in front of me. I show up in the moment with positivity.

- **Affection:** I treat myself with positive regard and *affection*. Through treating myself affectionately, I am able to express more positivity and be affectionate with others.

- **Action:** I move into *action* out of a centered place by taking time to pause and regenerate.

B

QUALITIES

Balance, Bravery, Beauty, Brilliance, Birth

SAMPLE AFFIRMATIONS

- **Balance:** I am filled with an understanding of my innate *balance*. I nourish my body, mind, and spirit by the healthy lifestyle that I live.

- **Bravery:** I practice *bravery* by letting go of what no longer serves me and by accepting the things I cannot change.

- **Beauty:** I am beautiful, and I see the inner *beauty* in myself and those around me.

- **Brilliance:** I affirm that this world is a place of *brilliance* and light. I shine my inner light in all that I do.

- **Birth:** I give *birth* to the me that I want to be, and I am good!

C

QUALITIES

Centered, Capable, Charming, Curious, Childlike

SAMPLE AFFIRMATIONS

- **Centered:** I move through the activities of each day from a *centered* space, taking time to pause and regenerate.

- **Capable:** I am *capable*. I speak to myself in loving ways and I honor the things I can do. Through recognizing my capabilities, I bring more positivity into my life and am eager to try new things.

- **Charming:** I am *charming*. I shine a pleasing bright light and draw to me the people and situations that serve my highest good.

- **Curious:** I am *curious* about life's great mystery. I embrace synchronicity and spontaneity—knowing that things happen in their own time and for my greatest good.

- **Childlike:** Jesus said to become like a child, as children more readily see the beauty in the world. Knowing this, I cherish the purity, innocence, and *childlike* spirit within me.

D

QUALITIES

Decisive, Deep, Devoted, Diligent, Direct

SAMPLE AFFIRMATIONS

- **Decisive:** I move with purpose in my life and being *decisive* gives me power. I recognize that no is a complete sentence, and that healthy boundaries serve my highest good.

- **Deep:** I honor the *deep* knowingness within me, recognizing that finding quiet time to center myself serves my highest good.

- **Devoted:** I am *devoted* to living my life to the fullest and I move with Divine Rhythm.

- **Diligent:** I am *diligent* in the way that I approach my spiritual practice, knowing that I have the power to make my life a heaven or a hell right here and right now.

- **Direct:** I communicate in a clear, concise, and *direct* way, knowing that the words I speak are truthful, loving, and consistent with my Highest Purpose.

E

QUALITIES

*Enthusiastic, Energetic, Easygoing,
Efficient, Emotion*

SAMPLE AFFIRMATIONS

- **Enthusiasm:** I meet the events of this day with a sense of *enthusiasm*, knowing that the best is yet to be.

- **Energetic:** It is okay for me to be *energetic* and to express positivity, for I am excited about life.

- **Easygoing:** I meet the obstacles I face with an *easygoing* attitude, knowing that everything is unfolding for my highest good.

- **Efficient:** I am *efficient*. I complete the tasks in front of me with purpose, direction, and vision.

- **Emotion:** I embrace the full realm of my human *emotions*, knowing that whatever arises will be healed in Divine Time. I trust in my own biology and affirm that all is well.

F

QUALITIES

Fastidious, Fabulous, Fervent,
Friendly, Funny

SAMPLE AFFIRMATIONS

- **Fastidious:** I am *fastidious* when it comes to my spiritual life, paying careful attention to my word, thought, and deed.

- **Fabulous:** I am absolutely *fabulous*, and I embrace myself as the wonderful spiritual being that I am.

- **Fervent:** I have a *fervent* spiritual vision, and I embrace my life with passion.

- **Friendly:** I am *friendly* to myself and friendly to others. I see the world as a friendly place, knowing that friendly attracts friendly. I draw friendship to me by the friendship I offer others.

- **Funny:** I have a good sense of humor and enjoy laughing and being *funny*.

- **Faith:** I trust life.

G

QUALITIES

*Generous, Gentle, Good,
Great, Gratitude*

SAMPLE AFFIRMATIONS

- **Generous:** I am *generous* with others and others are generous to me. The good that I give out comes back multiplied.

- **Gentle:** I treat myself *gently* and am *gentle* and kind in all of my relationships.

- **Goodness:** I embrace the *goodness* that is the living spirit within me.

- **Greatness:** I know that I am capable of accomplishing *great* things. I hold a high vision for myself and know that my good will positively affects others and the world at large. I recognize that even seemingly small acts of kindness are great, as they have a ripple effect.

- **Gratitude:** I have an "attitude of *gratitude*" and often think and/ or write down all of the things I am grateful for. I recognize that each moment is new. I can always start over.

H

QUALITIES

Heart-centered, Helpful, Highest Good, Holy, Helm

SAMPLE AFFIRMATIONS

- **Heart-centered:** I find my *heart-centered* nature through taking the time to pause and go within.
- **Helpful:** I am *helpful* to those in need and what I give out comes back multiplied.
- **Highest Good:** Everything is unfolding in divine right order. I embrace the idea that situations and circumstances are unfolding for my *Highest Good*. My life is a living prayer.
- **Holy:** I live my life in a *holy* way. I love myself and others, and I am a magnet for GOOD.
- **Helm:** I am at the *helm* of my life ship and I steer it toward the GOOD!

I

QUALITIES

Imagination, Independent, Inventive, Inspired, Intelligent

SAMPLE AFFIRMATIONS

- **Imagination:** I use my *imagination* to call love and light into my world. Even in my darkest hour, I know that the light will shine once more.

- **Independent:** I embrace my own *independence* and march to the beat of my own drummer. I trust that what no longer serves me will fall away.

- **Inventive:** I approach life with a sense of ingenuity and *inventiveness*. I am a creator in my own life and I choose to make it GOOD.

- **Inspired:** My life is Divinely *Inspired*. I give thanks to my teachers on the path and am grateful to know how to use my Divine Tools.

- **Intelligent:** I am *intelligent*. Like a snowflake, there is no one else like me. I am unique. I shine my love-light out into the world, trusting that Divine Intelligence heals all situations and circumstances.

J

QUALITIES

Juicy, Joyous, Just, Jazzed, Jubilant

SAMPLE AFFIRMATIONS

- **Juicy:** My life is *juicy* and overflows with sweetness. I trust in the sweetness of life itself.

- **Joyous:** I move toward what is *joyous* in life. I am a source of joy to others and others in turn bring me joy. If I don't feel it now, I trust that my season of joy will come. Godspeed.

- **Just:** I trust that the Universe is good and *just* and that everything unfolds in divine right order.

- **Jazzed:** I find reasons to be *jazzed* about life and move toward those who have an attitude of gratitude.

- **Jubilance:** I move toward what is *jubilant*. Even if I don't feel it now, I trust that a day of great happiness and triumph will come again. I trust the flow of life.

K

QUALITIES

Kindness, Keenness, Kinship

SAMPLE AFFIRMATIONS

- **Kindness:** My life is an expression of *kindness*. I express kindness to myself, others, and the environment.

- **Keenness:** I have a *keen* sense of what is good and right, and I move toward my GOOD.

- **Kinship:** I reach out to others in the spirit of *kinship*. I am a friend to others on this journey.

- **Knower:** I enter into relationships with the Divine Knower through my spiritual practices.

L

QUALITIES

Level-headed, Lovable, Likable, Lovely, Luminous

SAMPLE AFFIRMATIONS

- **Level-headed:** I am *level-headed* when I need to be, recognizing that this journey called life can be confusing. I trust my heart center and embrace divine right order.

- **Lovable:** I am *lovable*. I am a unique being who is worthy of love, independent of past mistakes. I forgive myself. I love myself.

- **Likable:** I am *likable*. I am a magnet for positivity.

- **Lovely:** I make my life and home environment *lovely*. My personal space is a source of comfort and I fill it with things that I love.

- **Luminous:** I am a light in my own life and in the lives of others. I shine with *luminosity*.

M

QUALITIES

Motivated, Miraculous, Magic, Magnificent, Meticulous

SAMPLE AFFIRMATIONS

- **Motivated:** I am *motivated* to show up for my own life with positivity and hope. I accept what is in front of me and embrace life's mysteries, knowing that all is well in the eyes of God.

- **Miraculous:** I affirm that life is indeed *miraculous*, and that situations and circumstances are unfolding for my Highest Good.

- **Magic:** I embrace the *magic* of healing and affirm that miracles are possible.

- **Magnificent:** I affirm that my existence is *magnificent*. I embody the good in all that I think, say, and do. Yes, today is a new day. I begin new!

- **Meticulous:** I am *meticulous* with my thought, word, and action—and am a peaceful presence on this earth.

N

QUALITIES

Natural, Noble, Nice, Newness

SAMPLE AFFIRMATIONS

- **Natural:** I move in sync with the natural world. I love Mother Earth and cherish her resources.

- **Noble:** I am *noble* in the way I relate to others. The ideals that I express are divine.

- **Nice:** I am nice to myself and *nice* to others. I emanate peace.

- **Newness:** I embrace *new* situations and circumstances, knowing that my Good is around the corner.

- **North Star:** My North Star shines on me as I commit to a spiritual practice.

O

QUALITIES

Offering, Opulent, Outgoing, Organic, Order

SAMPLE AFFIRMATIONS

- **Offering:** My life is a Divine *Offering* and I ask God each day how I can be of service to myself, others, and the environment.

- **Opulent:** The good that is available to me is *opulent* in the most divine sense of the word. My life is lavish as I luxuriate in God.

- **Outgoing:** I am motivated and *outgoing*, shining my light in all that I do.

- **Organic:** My life unfolds organically. I respect my connection to Mother Earth, and I allow my Good to unfold *organically* rather than trying to force things to happen.

- **Order:** I trust that my life is unfolding in divine right *order*, even when I can't see it.

- **Open:** I am open to learning and growing.

P

QUALITIES

Passionate, Peaceful, Persevering, Positive, Powerful

SAMPLE AFFIRMATIONS

- **Passionate:** I am *passionate* about life, and I allow Divine Passion to move through me as I inspire myself and others.

- **Peaceful:** I find what is *peaceful* by stopping, pausing, and looking within. From this place, I see the ever-present peace in the world around me.

- **Persevering:** When I experience life obstacles like grief, depression, or sadness, I *persevere*, knowing that there is light at the end of the tunnel. I *persevere* in the pursuit of my dreams knowing that in God anything is possible.

- **Positive:** I am a *positive* person, knowing that Goodness is always at hand. I trust that everything is unfolding for my good even when I can't see it.

- **Powerful:** I am beautiful and *powerful*. I embrace my true Power knowing that the living spirit guides me in all that I think, say, and do. All I have to do is call on it!

Q

QUALITIES

Quality, Quick, Quiet, Quirky

SAMPLE AFFIRMATIONS

- **Quality:** My life is high-*quality* as I discover the qualities inside myself and my own name and use them to manifest my greatest good.

- **Quick:** I am *quick* to see my life as good, and to weed out negative thinking that no longer serves me.

- **Quiet:** I find *quiet* and peace within, knowing Divine Quiet is ever-present, even when I can't see it.

- **Quirky:** I embrace my unique *quirkiness* and use what is unique about me for my highest good.

- **Quest:** I am grateful for my spiritual quest which grounds me.

R

QUALITIES

Reassuring, Resourceful, Responsible, Reverent, Regenerative

SAMPLE AFFIRMATIONS

- **Reassuring:** When I have doubts, I remind and *reassure* myself that the Universe is GOOD.

- **Resourceful:** I am *resourceful*. I use the resources available to me to make positive changes in my life. I continue to reach toward the good even in my darkest hours, knowing that God is an ever-present resource, even when I don't see it.

- **Responsible:** I am *responsible* by creating a healthy life for myself and facing what is in front of me.

- **Reverent:** I am filled with a *reverence* for life and give thanks for being alive.

- **Regenerative:** I take time each day to pause and *regenerate*.

- **Responsive:** I choose to respond with calm and focus rather than react.

S

QUALITIES

Strength, Serenity, Sincere, Synchronistic, Sober

SAMPLE AFFIRMATIONS

- **Strength:** By taking time to pause and regenerate, I increase my *strength*.

- **Serenity:** As they say in twelve-step groups, I find *serenity* through accepting the things I cannot change. I know that God or the Universe readily offers me this serenity.

- **Sincere:** I am *sincere* to myself and others—and know this as I move into action.

- **Synchronistic:** I embrace life's *synchronicities* and seeming coincidences, knowing that I am being led by an ever-loving presence.

- **Sober:** I live a life *sober* from addictive behavior. I know that, if I have a desire to remove an addiction from my life, it will be removed.

T

QUALITIES

Talented, Truthful, Thoughtful, Tolerant, Tactful

SAMPLE AFFIRMATIONS

- **Talented:** I am *talented*. I honor myself for what I am able to do well—and I know that I have unique talents that I have yet to discover.

- **Truthful:** I live a life centered in Divine *Truth* and am conscious of this *truth* in thought, word, and action.

- **Thoughtful:** I am *thoughtful* of myself as well as others as I move through life. And as it is written, I do unto others as I would have them do unto me.

- **Tolerant:** I am *tolerant* of others who do not hold my views.

- **Tactful:** I am *tactful* and diplomatic in the way I advocate for myself and others, knowing that my words have a ripple effect.

U

QUALITIES

*Unbound, Uncommon, Unaffected,
Understanding, Unconditional*

SAMPLE AFFIRMATIONS

- **Unbound:** I am *unbound*! I take time to pause, regenerate, and free myself from worry.

- **Uncommon:** I am unique and *uncommon*. I embrace my originality. There is no one like me on this planet.

- **Unaffected:** Jesus said, be in the world but not of the world. I am *unaffected* by external situations and circumstances, knowing that I am guided by the good of this Universe.

- **Understanding:** I have compassion and *understanding* for the suffering within myself as well as the suffering of others.

- **Unconditional:** I practice giving *unconditional* love to myself. I love myself no matter where I am in my healing process.

V

QUALITIES

Versatile, Valuable, Vivacious, Vibrate, Validation

SAMPLE AFFIRMATIONS

- **Versatile:** I am *versatile* in my approach to life and in relationships, understanding that we are all on our own unique journeys. When I am hurting, I focus on what I can and can't change in myself and the world around me.

- **Valuable:** I am *valuable* and offer my unique qualities to the world.

- **Vivacious:** I approach life with a sense of excitement, expectancy, and vivaciousness, knowing that the best is yet to be.

- **Vibrate:** I *vibrate* at a high frequency, knowing that the thoughts I think create the quality of my experience.

- **Validation:** I know that true *validation* comes from self-love. I validate myself, knowing that I am on the right path.

W

QUALITIES

Wonder, Warm-hearted, Willing, Well-behaved

SAMPLE AFFIRMATIONS

- **Wonder:** I know that good comes when I am willing to approach life with a sense of childlike *wonder*. Life is a wonder, and I approach it knowing that all is well when I see with God's eyes.

- **Warm-hearted:** I am *warm-hearted* and see things from a variety of perspectives. With a loving attitude I am of service to those in need.

- **Willing:** I am *willing* to grow and change. I am willing to learn and grow through my grief and suffering, knowing that all is ultimately well, even when I can't see it.

- **Well-behaved:** I am *well-behaved* in difficult life circumstances. I practice self-control when needed, and I speak out when needed. I listen to the voice within before acting. I forgive myself and others for past transgressions. I recognize that being *well-behaved* comes by first learning to treat myself kindly.

X

QUALITIES

Xenial, Xenodochial, Extraordinary, Expectant

SAMPLE AFFIRMATIONS

- **Xenial:** I am a host- or hostess-with-the-mostest and treat my guests like gold. I keep my heart open and treat others as I would like to be treated.

- **Xenodochial:** I am friendly to the stranger, knowing that we are all God's children. I keep my heart open in difficult times.

- **Extraordinary:** There is only one me. My life is *extraordinary*.

- **Expectant:** I am *expectant* of my Good, knowing that the Universe is full of wonderful surprises. In the darkest of times, I urge myself to expect the Good that awaits.

Y

QUALITIES

Yielding, Yogic, Youthful, Yummy

SAMPLE AFFIRMATIONS

- **Yielding:** I am *yielding* like a rock in the ocean, allowing the Universe to carve me to its liking. I am open to Divine Possibilities.

- **Yogic:** I approach life with the wisdom of a *yogi*, treating my body like a temple, knowing that peace is found by going within.

- **Youthful:** I approach life with a sense of *youthful* vigor, keeping my heart open wide and taking time to honor the ever-changing *youthful* spirit within. I parent the child within when I feel wounded, knowing that self-love heals.

- **Yummy:** Life is *yummy*, and I am open to Divine Possibilities. I splash in the divine water of life. As Ram Dass says, "Yum! Yum! Yum!"

Z

QUALITIES

Zealous, Zany, Zestful, Zippy

SAMPLE AFFIRMATIONS

- **Zealous:** I approach life with excitement and *zeal*.
- **Zany:** I embrace my uniqueness and eccentricities. I am *zany*, fun, and alive in my uniqueness. Like a snowflake, there is only one me, and I choose to love me.
- **Zestful:** My life is filled with *zest* and I spice things up when needed.
- **Zippy:** I am like the song *Zip-a-Dee-Doo-Dah*. "My, Oh, My, what a wonderful day!" I embrace my inner *zippiness*.
- **Zen:** I find moments of quiet and focused Zen each day.

Acknowledgments

Many thanks for the diverse spiritual communities and teachings to which I feel a connection. And a heartfelt high-five to all who honor our precious daughter's memory by supporting The Kara Love Project. Thank you to Joey Lugassy for lugging your harmonium each week for two months through Cedars Sinai and chanting Kirtan at my bedside while I lay there on mandatory bed rest. And to Micheline Berry for your sisterhood and the magical orchid plant that kept me company during those humdrum hospital days. A big wave to the Thursday ladies and my sponsors past and present for helping to keep me sober and sane. You show up and sustain life. To the late Dr. Bob Friedland. Thank you for delivering our angel into this world. You are missed. A special shoutout to the OGs: Narayan Zalben, Badri Margolin and the whole mishpocha, Govind Das and Radha, and Shiva Baum and family. You are our Bhakti Family. Thank you for offering space in your homes and hearts over the years. You have ever so gently taught me the power of Guru Grace. To Jesse, Owen, Auntie Jane Watkins, Shelley Karpaty and family, and Uncles Howard and John—our surrogate family—you are so dear to us. To Mark Whitwell for teaching me to be with my breath and embodiment through Yoga. And to all those friends and teachers who have found their way onto the path: Dr. Connie Corley, Julie Devi Hale, Josh Brill, Spring Gross, Alisa Ruby Bash, Tracy Milan, Connie Corley, Felicia Tomasko, Zoe Kors, David Stringer, Dearbhla Kelly, Winter, and Brendan, plus too many more to mention.

Thank you to my editor, Andrea Cagan, who believed in my message and my first 20,000 words and helped me to integrate the next

20,000. I could not have done it without you. To my agent Gareth Esersky, to Brenda Knight and everyone at Mango, and to Tanya Ferrell for your guidance. To my friend and mentor Judith Orloff for your unwavering support and belief in my voice and to Corey Folsom for your gentle wisdom. To Lorin Roche, Camille Maurine, Denise Kaufman, Marianne Williamson, Sharon Salzberg, and Trudy Goodman, thank you for signing on from the start and giving wings to my work in your own unique ways. Your support shone light on this project in those moments of self-doubt. To Michael Beckwith and Rickie Byars for carrying me when I was knocked to my knees (on more occasions than you even know) and for your ongoing love and friendship. To Julie Lear, my BFF of over thirty years. This work would not be possible without your love, hands-on support and willingness to listen. You continue to teach me the importance of living in integrity and of the power of love and friendship. It is a joy to walk this path with you. Thank you for all that you do to support and guide this endeavor. To my sister Mary Ann for her love and forgiveness, my brother-in-law Andy, and to my niece and nephew Sophie and Zack. I can never forget the Epstein, Edelstein, Ziaee, Srenco, and Nevins families. And many thanks to my parents Ken and Nancy who were my very first teachers, and the loving memory of Granny Myrt and Grandpa Al, and Grandma Marcie and Grandpa Mickey (Meyer). To Rabbi Neil Comess-Daniels and his wife Toby who helped me to find the beauty in reconnecting to Judaism in my own unique way. You are precious to our family. Thank you to friend and artist, Torie Zalben, to know you is to love you. May we continue to champion each other and shine on. To Ruthie D. and Debby P. for your love and friendship. To the DeVaul family, the Rufeh family, the Weitzman, Wilson, Levin, Rubin, Klein, and Henderson families. To Mimi and G. and Hillary C. and family; and to all the families who we get to express the joy of being parents with. You know who you are. To Cristina Pereza, Heidi

Beuch, Angelica Von Seyfried, Kelly Mickel, The Unatti Girls, and to all my mentors in the not for profit world. Thank you for your help in making this Vision manifest! May we continue to champion each other and shine on! To Matt Daley and the Daley Clan, our friends for over thirty years and the birthday crew: Coley, Yana, Monica, and Dustin. To Jim and Kathy Dulan and to James Dulan who I never had the honor to meet. To my daughters Sally and Marcelle. You are precious beyond measure. And last but not least to my husband David, who has taught me most everything I know about the power of forgiveness, patience, selflessness, and unconditional love.

About the Author

Lily Dulan is an MFT Psychotherapist with a Master's Degree in Psychology and a Master of Fine Arts in Creative Writing from Antioch University, Los Angeles. She played an instrumental role in starting the LGBTQ Affirmative Psychology Specialization at Antioch University and holds a Master of Arts Degree in Teaching from Simmons College in Boston, Massachusetts. Lily is a certified Heart of Yoga Teacher and Bhakti Yogini. She studied Spiritual Coursework at Agape International Spiritual Center under the tutelage of Reverend Michael Bernard Beckwith.

Drawing on her studies of both Eastern and Western disciplines, she created a heart-centered system of healing she calls The Name Work. After her first daughter, Kara Meyer Dulan, died at home from SIDS at two months old, she started a foundation in her memory called The Kara Love Project. She has teamed up with international organizations such as the Unatti Foundation in Nepal and local nonprofits such as Venice Arts and Foster Nation in Los Angeles to serve marginalized youth. Lily also facilitates workshops at her home in Los Angeles where she hosts a variety of educational and charitable events. She lives in Los Angeles with her husband, David, and her two daughters.

Mango Publishing, established in 2014, publishes an eclectic list of books by diverse authors—both new and established voices—on topics ranging from business, personal growth, women's empowerment, LGBTQ studies, health, and spirituality to history, popular culture, time management, decluttering, lifestyle, mental wellness, aging, and sustainable living. We were recently named 2019 *and* 2020's #1 fastest growing independent publisher by *Publishers Weekly.* Our success is driven by our main goal, which is to publish high-quality books that will entertain readers as well as make a positive difference in their lives.

Our readers are our most important resource; we value your input, suggestions, and ideas. We'd love to hear from you—after all, we are publishing books for you!

Please stay in touch with us and follow us at:

Facebook: Mango Publishing
Twitter: @MangoPublishing
Instagram: @MangoPublishing
LinkedIn: Mango Publishing
Pinterest: Mango Publishing
Newsletter: mangopublishinggroup.com/newsletter

Join us on Mango's journey to reinvent publishing, one book at a time.